SHEAD RANCH CEMETERY

1800s TEXAS

M M Walker
with A M Walker

Copyright © 2014 M M WALKER
All rights reserved.
ISBN-13: 978-0692231814
ISBN-10: 0692231811

SHEAD RANCH CEMETERY

1800s TEXAS
A LIMESTONE & McLENNAN COUNTIES CEMETERY

ACKNOWLEDGEMENT
Joel P Shedd II (1906-1982)

A lawyer and researcher, Joel began a genealogy quest that took him many wonderful places. He served as vice chairman of the Armed Services Board of Contract Appeals and was on the Georgia and DC bars. He published law reviews that are still being referenced today. Genealogy became a hobby sparked by assisting his wife in searching for her family origin and grew to a passion. His lasting legacy of this desire to know more of his family history continues to benefit the generations that have followed him. I am grateful for his curiosity and perseverance. The work he left for us is in his book, "The Shedd Family of the Southern States Descended from James Shed of Loudoun County, Virginia". Locating a copy of this book has been an interesting quest, and the book was instrumental in providing direction along my journey.

A Note of Thanks
To the Central Texas Genealogy Society for permission to use their survey information, to Linda Jordan and Bruce Jordan for permission to use the information from their survey, and to the Williamson Creek Baptist Church Brotherhood for their invaluable restoration work.

Contents

Founding of a Texas Cattle Ranch and Frontier Cemetery 5
Shed Lineage and Many Ways to Spell a Name 11
Census, Agriculture Schedules and Surveys 17
    Shead Ranch Cemetery Surveys 21
Characteristics of an 1800's Frontier Cemetery
    Before Undertakers and Funeral Parlors 25
SHEAD FAMILY PROFILES 37
    SHEAD 37
    CHILDREN OF J M SHEID, SHEID MCKINNEY Siblings 42
    SANDERSON 45
    HENRY 47
    THOMPSON 49
    LYON WALKER WOOD 51
    ROBISON 53
AREA FAMILY PROFILES 57
    A through G 57
    DAVIS 67
    H through W 69
MAPS and Marker Locations 73
Research and Preservation notes: 89
    2013 90
    2014 92
Marker Photographs 97
Bibliography 121
Index 122

INTRODUCTION

How the Shed Family was Brought to America

We trace our family's arrival in America back to the Scottish Record Office entry of 1749, when the parents of James Shed, age 14, and William Shed, age 6, report that their children have been stolen. Along with 28 other Scottish boys, they are transported aboard the Aberdeen Queen, bound for Dumfries, Virginia, and indentured slavery. James survives and raises three sons west of Washington. The second generation, William, James Thompson, and George, move their families to South Carolina. William serves in the American Revolution. Of the third generation, James serves in the War of 1812. His son, James Austin Shed, and the grandson of William of the American Revolution, William Robertson Shead, will move their families to Texas.

A cemetery is a gift of knowledge placed as prominently as possible for future generations so that they might know who was here before. Historians, anthropologists and archaeologists rely on what their work finds and on what the living choose to leave for future generations. The oldest structure known to exist today is the Carin of Barnenez, ca 4800 BC, a type of passage tomb that contains chiseled engravings of debatable meaning. From the Egyptian pyramid of Djosher, built around 2600 BC, and those of Giza, the center of a royal cemetery outward to the mastabas, tombs of nobles, and on to the painted caves that hold the markings left for generations that would follow, we see what the living chose to leave as a reminder of their lives thousands of years ago.

It is in these places that we learn the customs lost through time, the names of the dead and what they wanted us to know about them and their lives. In the Shead Ranch Cemetery, so recent in comparison, we find family relationships, friendships and messages of love. The evidence is carved in stone, shown in the nearness of plots and stories are told in the words and dates left for us.

Founding of a Texas Cattle Ranch and Frontier Cemetery

During the time that Texas is a territory of Spain, James Manson Sheid and his wife, Sibbel Robertson Sheid, move through Georgia from South Carolina, and then finally to Coffee County Tennessee. They raise four sons and one daughter, the eldest sons being William Robertson Shead and Manson Sheid. In approximately 1834, William and Manson venture to *Coahuila y Tejas*, the Mexican territory of Texas, leaving William's young wife with his parents in the safety and stability of America.

Manson works as a carpenter in San Augustine, just west of the Sabine River. William apprentices with a lawyer in Liberty, 140 miles south of his brother.

When the majority of American immigrants residing in Texas revolt against Mexican rule, William first enlists with the town's defense, the Liberty Safety Committee, and then rides to battle in Bexar, the location now known as San Antonio in Bexar County. On later papers filed as Claims of the Republic, he is identified as riding to the Campaign of Bexar, and following documents state he is there to participate in the Siege of Bexar.

Manson enlists on December 14, 1835, and serves in Bexar defending the Alamo. He is in Captain William Carey's artillery company. Manson dies in the siege of that mission on March 6, 1836.

William's record shows that he stayed in Bexar through December of 1835, when others of the Liberty group with whom he'd ridden leave the area of the siege. Without his brother, he goes back to his family in Tennessee and completes his law studies. In 1850, he starts a journey: a permanent move to Texas via Arkansas, traveling with many other family members, including his cousin, James Austin Shed. James and William may have made exploratory trips to Texas before bringing their extensive families with the mission of locating land suitable for ranching.

James Austin Shed and his family settle in Shelby County on the eastern border of Texas. He and his children establish a cattle ranch along the Flat Fork River.

William Robertson Shead explores westward. He soon chooses land on the border of McLennan and

Limestone counties. William begins the long process of arranging for surveys and applying for land grants even while his family is constructing homes and beginning to build cattle herds.

The land grants, the right to claim government-owned land for a small fee, vary in size and are categorized by the requirements to be met by people applying for such grants. A Headrights grant is given to people in the area that would become the Republic of Texas before 1837. Military grants are based on service dates in the militia of the rebellion and within the ranks of the Republic's army. Special circumstances also allow for land grants based on service to the Republic such as David Crockett of Tennessee, who was instrumental in the rebellion, but insisted on remaining a private citizen.

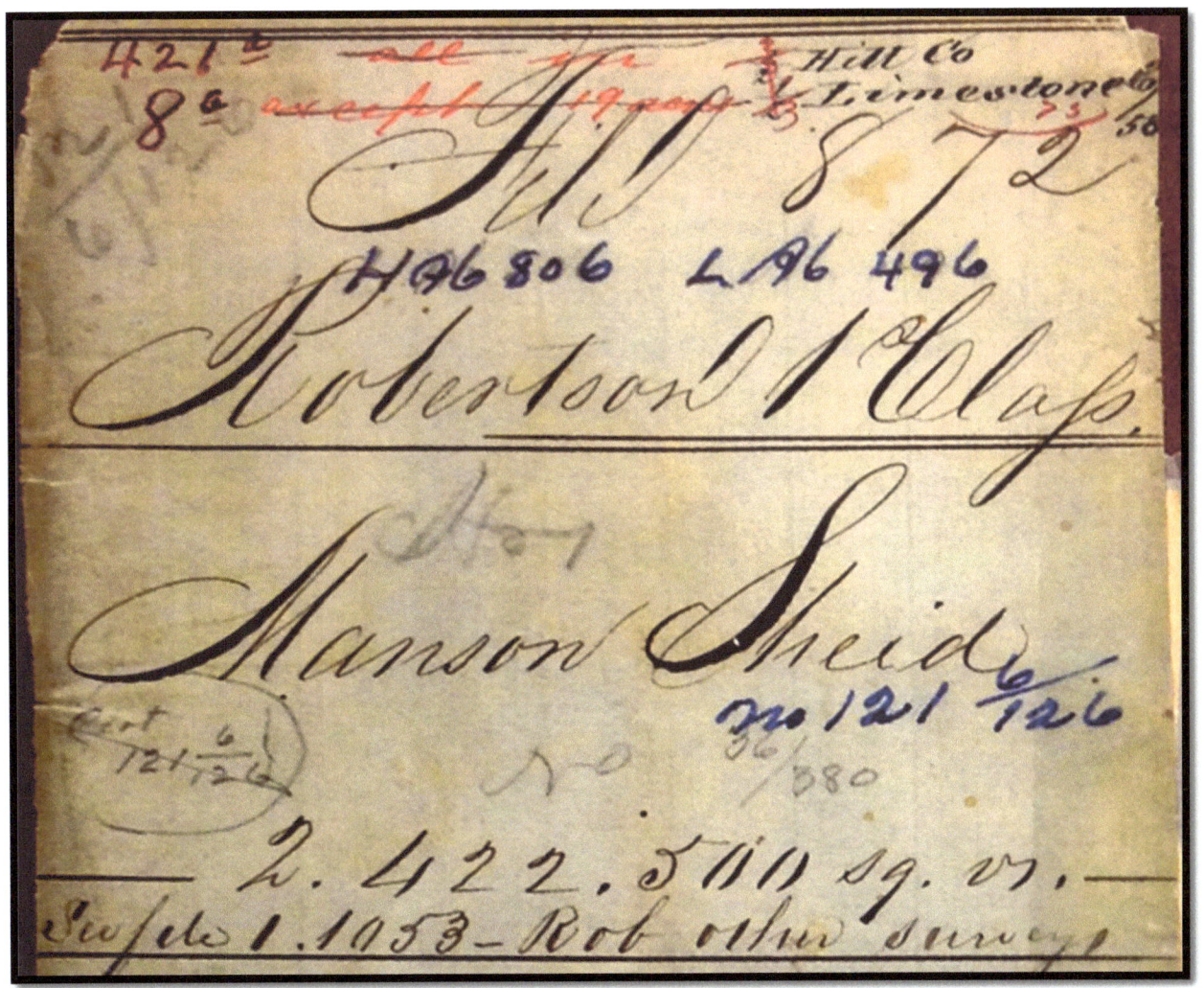

Other states held land lotteries to encourage settlement of immigrants from the east or granted land rights based on other criteria, such as surveying and military service. William's applications for land grants are based on Headrights grants for himself and Manson as well as Manson's enlisted military service during the Texas Revolution.

In Texas, the process of claiming land can take many years. An applicant must have a certificate granting the right to a set amount of land. They then hold a patent, or exclusive right to claim that amount of land. They must provide a survey of the land they want to claim and verify through the land office that the land is not already owned. The land will then be recorded as owned by the patentee, who then is registered as the grantee. The cemetery is on the western end of the main section of the ranch, defined by two patents, one in William's name and the other in Manson's. The borders of the cemetery are within patent A-507. William is both the patentee and grantee for this Headrights land. The eastern end of this portion of the ranch is registered as patented to the heirs of Manson Sheid, and the grant is recorded simply in his name, not as being granted to his heirs. His heirs have the right to claim land which is then owned by Manson's estate.

The original survey for William's Headrights grant stretches along the border of McLennan and Limestone, straddling both sides of that line. The land he surveys and files a patent for based on Manson's service and Headrights is contained in Limestone and Hill counties. The central portion of the ranch equals 1400 acres. Other sections that are not connected to the central portion total approximately 800 acres.

The cemetery is established within the central portion of the ranch, just west of the McLennan county line. It is about 150 feet inside Limestone County. Near the end of the 20th century, the location and conservation of the cemetery fell into dispute. Texas Land Commission records and maps certify that the cemetery is within the boundary of Limestone County. Several of the people interred in the cemetery lived in McLennan County, and the Fall and Puckett funeral homes that conducted many of the services in later decades were also within McLennan, so the confusion is easy to understand.

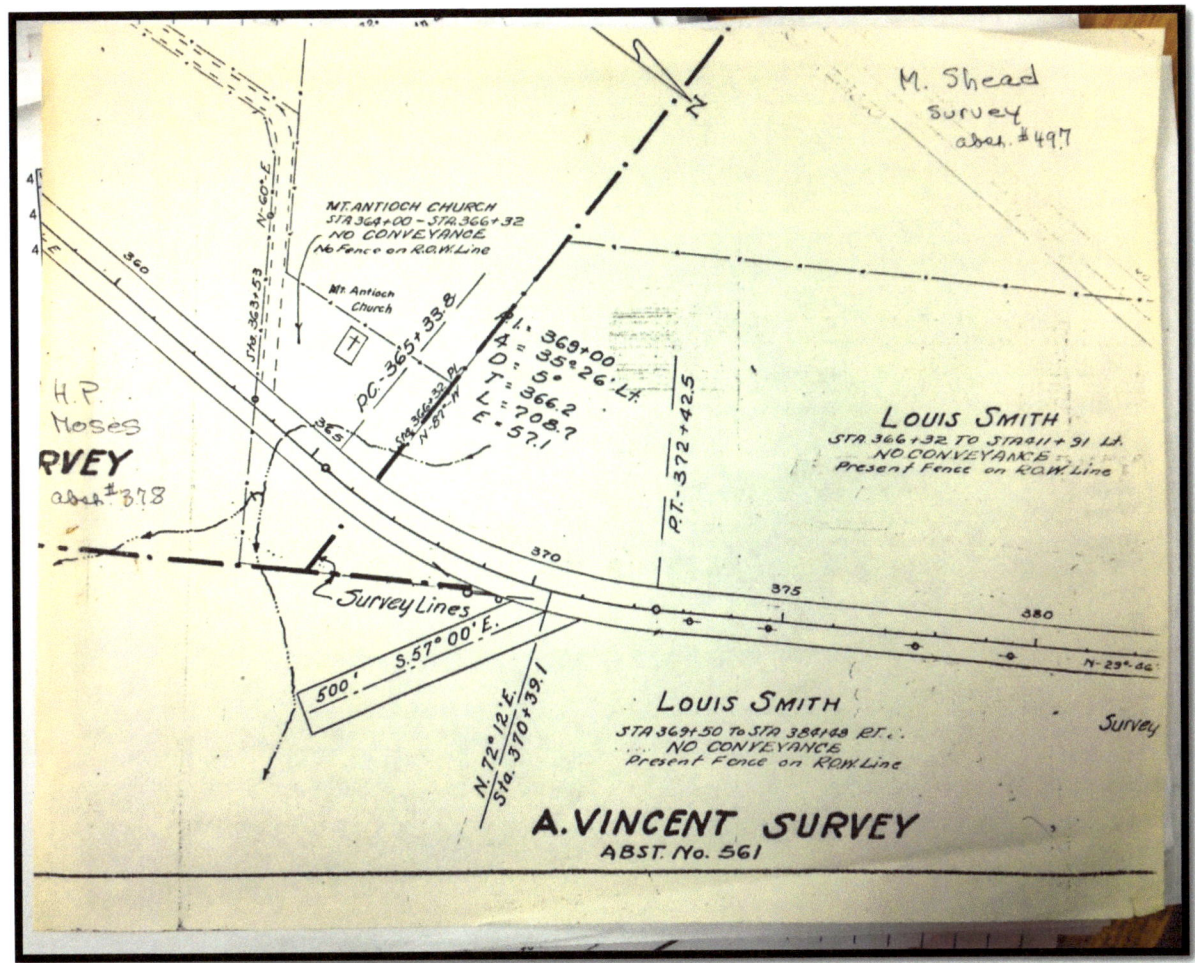

    The A. Vincent Survey shows one of the three northern sections of the ranch. This location is primarily used for raising horses. The center of this survey will become the small community of Mount Antioch, located halfway between the main section of the ranch and Mount Calm, which borders Hill County.

    Though the map labels the section as M. Shead, Abstract 497, the patent was granted to Manson Sheid Heirs. A community cemetery is established west of the church.

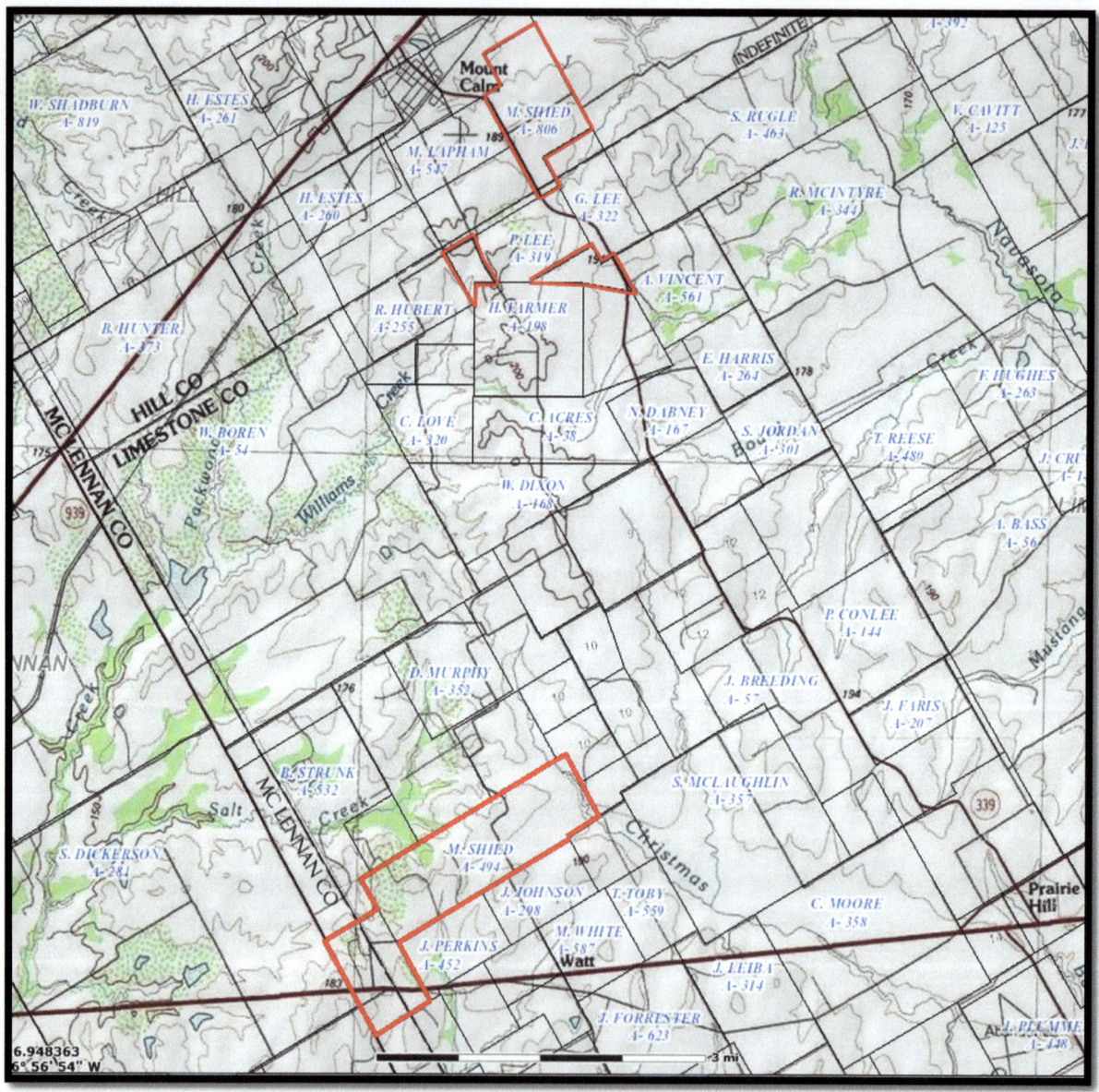

Texas General Land Office map depicting all portions of land granted in McLennan, Limestone, and Hill Counties.
Blue font depicts original land grant names and abstract numbers.

Shed Lineage and Many Ways to Spell a Name

The original spelling of the name is that report filed in 1749 in Aberdeen, Scotland, recording the abduction of two brothers, William and James Shed. The first generation born in America to the eldest of these Scottish boys, William, James Thompson and George, move their families to South Carolina. William serves in the American Revolution. Of the second and third American generation, James serves in the War of 1812. His son, James Austin Shed, and the grandson of William of the American Revolution, William Robertson Shead will move their families to Texas.

Spelling of last names vary depending on the census taker, the court clerk, registrar for marriage licenses and region of residence. In Scotland's Record Office, we found "Shed," and in America, the spelling varies by generation, location, and even among siblings.

The kidnapped child, James of Aberdeen, Scotland, spelled his name Shed on a land lease he signed as recorded in the Virginia Deed book G pp. 49-53, "*Ashton to Shed*", as did his sons. American Revolutionary War veteran, William, the eldest son of James of Aberdeen, spelled his name Shed on his military documents, but the next generation began to vary the spelling.

William Robertson's father and siblings used the spelling Sheid. It also appears on some records for this generation as Shedd. The spelling of William Robertson's last name at birth was Sheid and appears as Shed on Texas Revolution era documents, and later as Shead when he has completed his law studies. His children use Shead as the preferred spelling. William's cousin, James Austin Shed used the original spelling, but many of his children, including two who were Texas Frontier Rangers in Titus County, spelled their name Shedd on the roster of their troop. In the Shead Ranch Cemetery, there is a child's headstone bearing the spelling Sheid, a niece of William's.

The Texas General Land Office (GLO) has variations from Shead to Sheid and Shied. The last, Shied, is a clerk's transposition error that occurred sometime after original documents of 1840 were filed, but remains as a cross indexed spelling in the GLO as well as records at the Alamo to this day. The jacket for file 872 at the GLO for Robertson's 1st Class Headrights has the spelling of Manson Sheid. This document references land grants for Limestone and Hill Counties.

For Manson, who died at the Alamo, the spelling preferred by his father, which is Sheid, should be used.

The following map drawn in 1858 by the Texas General Land Office depicts the correct spelling of Sheid for the tract of land granted to heirs of Manson Sheid. The transposition error of Sheid to Shied occurred some time after 1858.

Limestone County Survey from GLO   1858

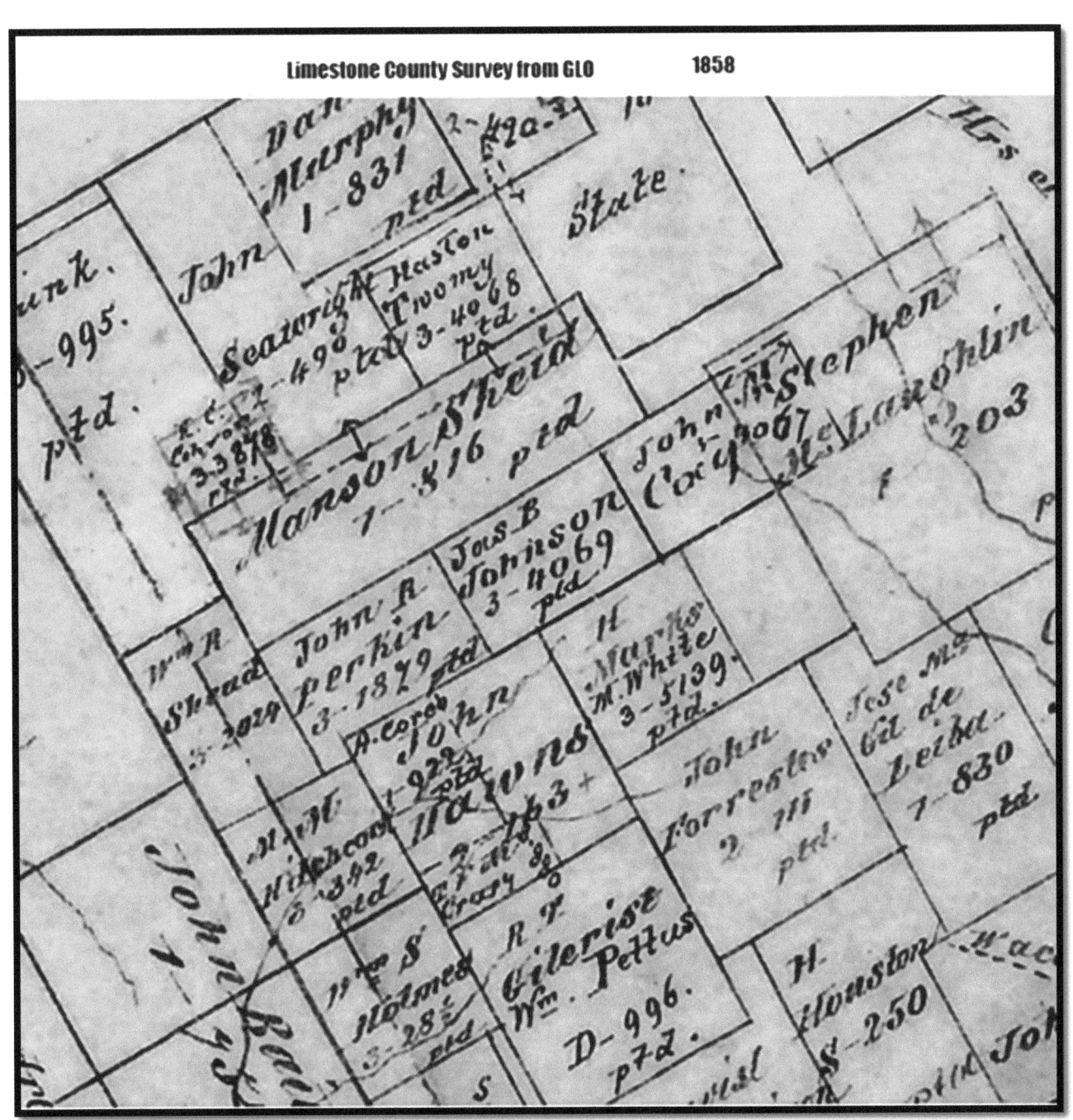

*The following is a list of the Sheid family of the third American generation that resided in Tennessee, the children descended from **James Manson Sheid** and **Sibbel Robertson Sheid**. Children and grand-children listed are known to have survived past childhood.*

1. **Nancy M Sheid** 1804 - 1839 married Thomas Robert Carl and had Elizabeth 1824 - 1896, James Harvey 1826 - 1911, Manson Augustus 1830 - 1912, Barton Arnold 1832 - 1915, Thomas Robert 1834 - 1917 and Jessie Jenkins 1837 - 1927.

2. **William Robertson Shead** 1807 - 1885, who we will follow to Texas, married Amanda *Graham* and had children listed in the next section.

3. **Manson Sheid** 1811 - 1835, single, died at the Alamo.

4. **Jesse J Sheid** 1812 - 1870 married Cynthia *Hamlet* and had Sarah Coziah *Sheid* Camp 1837 - 1888.

5. **James Manson Sheid II** 1816 - 1907 married Margaret B Sims and had Nancy *Sheid* Clark, 1843 - 1918, Jane J *Sheid* McKinney 1843 - 1918 and Julius C Sheid 1850 - 1918.

6. **Henry S Sheid** 1827 - 1911 married Mary E Patton and had Selina *Sheid* Taylor 1850 - 1878, Mary Clementine *Sheid* Gunn 1853 - 1935, Nancy Cora *Sheid* Willis 1858 - 1902, Jesse L *Sheid* Renick 1863 - 1943 and William Thomas Sheid 1864 - 1945.

(1) Nancy's husband moves east with his children after her early death.

(2) William's children settle in Texas.

(3) Jesse's daughter, Sara, visits the Texas ranch on several occasions.

(5) James M Sheid II's daughter, Jane, settles on the ranch, and his son, Julius, lives on the ranch in the Mount Calm area.

(6) Henry resides on the central portion of the ranch and has a cattle brand registered with Limestone County. He continues to maintain a residence in Tennessee. He finally retires in Texas to live with his son, William Thomas.

The children of **William Robertson Shead** and **Amanda Graham Shead** are as follows:

1. **Nancy Matilda** 1831 - 1900 married Morris Joseph Sanderson and had Edmond Ward 1851 -1911, William R 1854 - 1939, James Morris 1856 - 1915 and Joseph 1859.
2. **James B** 1833 - 1882 married Esther Richards and had Caledonia 1855 - 1906, Effie 1857 - 1857, Mary Ann 1859 - 1940 and Virginia 1861 - 1874.
3. **Mary Ann** 1834 - 1920 married Joel G Henry and had Celista 1856 - 1868, Laura 1858 - 1910, Joann 1861 - 1863, William 1864, John 1867, Charles 1870 - 1947, Nannie 1872 - 1962 and James 1876 -1878.
4. **Sibbel** 1835 - 1893 married William Magale and had Bill 1855 and Mary 1855.
5. **Margaret M** 1837 - 1852 single.
6. **Charles Baldwin** 1839 - 1925 married Mary Lucinda Bennett and had William 1869, James Benton 1872 - 1940, Charles 1897 and George 1882 - 1884.
7. **Thomas B** 1844 - 1864 single.
8. **Cassandra L** 1846 -1819 married Moses Palmer Coates and had Laura 1870, Frank 1871 - 1962 and William 1874.
9. **Amanda M** 1848 - 1870 married James C Coates and had Earnest 1870 - 1947.
10. **Manson H** 1850 - 1923 married Agnes A Lasswell and had Mattie 1873 -1950, Thomas 1898 - 1952, Edmond 1879 - 1880, Harvey 1882 - 1962, Mary 1887 - 1950, Mayme 1889 - 1964 and Katheryn 1892 - 1990.
11. **Laura Jane** 1853 -1933 married Charles E Sanderson and had Ellie 1879 - 1940 and James 1889 - 1958.

In his will, William leaves the ranch and cemetery to his children and grandchildren, dividing it nine ways between (1) Nancy, (2) the children of James B, (3) Mary Ann, (4) the children of Sibbel, (5) Charles B, (6) Cassandra L, (7) the daughter of Amanda M, (8) Manson H, and (9) Laura Jane. As the inheritors moved away and sold their portion of the ranch, they stipulated that the cemetery remained unsold.

Census, Agriculture Schedules and Surveys

Landscape

The central portion of the ranch which includes the cemetery sprawls across the line between McLennan and Limestone. The geological description of the Limestone side surrounding the cemetery uses the label "Normangee". This type of soil is primarily suited for cattle grazing. It has a moderate slope and drains well after a good rain.

The native plants are thin post oaks with Indian Grass, Switch Grass and Blue Grama grass that grow well in the open fields. Cedar trees do not proliferate in this region until annual wildfires are slowed by road development. The older generations tell stories of "when the cedars came up from Mexico", a major change to the environment, and a source of building material and firewood.

Wildflowers are abundant in late spring, and the cemetery is often blanketed with color from April through June. Bluebonnets, the state flower, grow particularly well in this soil.

Today, the major use of the land is still cattle ranching. Wildlife proliferates, and bird hunting is a tourist attraction. State-run facilities in the central portion of the ranch license and maintain bird hunting in season.

Limestone quarries are found to the north and east of the ranch.

Census

    US Federal entries of the Shead Ranch founder begin in Tennessee. William R Shead, on the 1840 US Federal census, is listed as residing in Marion County, Tennessee. One male under 5, one between 5 and 10, and himself between 30 and 40. Females, two under 5 years old, one between 5 and 10, and his wife, Amanda, is between 20 and 30.

    Though James Austin Shed has an 1850 US census entry, William R Shead does not. Both families begin the move west following the census-taking of that year.

William R Shead, listed on the 1860 Agriculture schedule (A county census of all agricultural business) of McLennan, has 316 acres of land, 40 of them described as being improved. He has less than a hundred cattle on this parcel of land. In Limestone County, on the same schedule, William has 1065 acres, of which 65 are improved. He pays taxes on 200 head of cattle in Limestone.

William's eldest son, James B Shead, listed on the 1860 Agriculture schedule of McLennan, has 3 acres of land, all of them improved. Taxed at $2585, this small acreage has a higher value than much larger plots. He has a large cattle herd.

William's second eldest son, Charles B Shead, on the 1860 Limestone County Agriculture schedule, has 120 acres of land that are not connected to the central portion of the ranch, but are north, near Mount Antioch and Mount Calm. In this general vicinity, the ranch has three portions of land, one stretching into Hill County. He has a herd of 20 cattle. More significantly, he has 30 horses, which would indicate his business is horse breeding. Charles stays close to Mount Calm and takes a mild interest in politics, eventually running for mayor in the first election of that community.

Approximately twenty years after establishing the ranch, on the 1870 US Census for Limestone County, William Robertson and Amanda have two children living at home with them; Manson H Shead, born 1851 in Arkansas, and his sister Laura Jane, born 1853 in Texas. Laura, later known as Janie, is the first Shead recorded to be born on the ranch. This census confirms that the family traveled through Arkansas to the home of Seaborn Shed, uncle to William R Shead and James Austin Shed, before crossing into Texas

The 1880 census will begin to show farmers in the area. Occupations expand to include teachers, doctors and dry goods merchants.

Shead Ranch Cemetery Surveys

In 1977, the McLennan County Historic Society conducts a survey of the Shead Ranch cemetery. Vernie S. Bennett of Mexia walks through the cemetery and records all information she can find. She locates and records 70 interments, including infants that share headstones with a parent.

Her survey is published in the Central Texas Genealogical compilation of Cemeteries of Limestone County, volume II, pages 562 and 563. Today, those important early records are maintained by the Central Texas Genealogy Society, headquartered in Waco.

In August of 2003, Bruce Jordan and Linda Jordan of Limestone undertake a survey of the Shead Ranch cemetery. They photograph headstones and notate epitaphs. During their work, they locate sixty-

four interments, including unnamed infants.

The missing six from the 1977 survey are accounted for with the removal of one that was erected pre-need, an overturned double monument that obscures the listing of an infant interment visible in 1977, markers that had been covered by shifting soil, and some that had toppled and crumbled. Transcription errors account for at least one on the 1977 survey, recorded without the later tools available such as digital photography and mobile computers.

Vernie Bennett accomplished a difficult task, and her published work established an early and very important record. The work done by Bruce and Linda was wide in scope and carefully detailed.

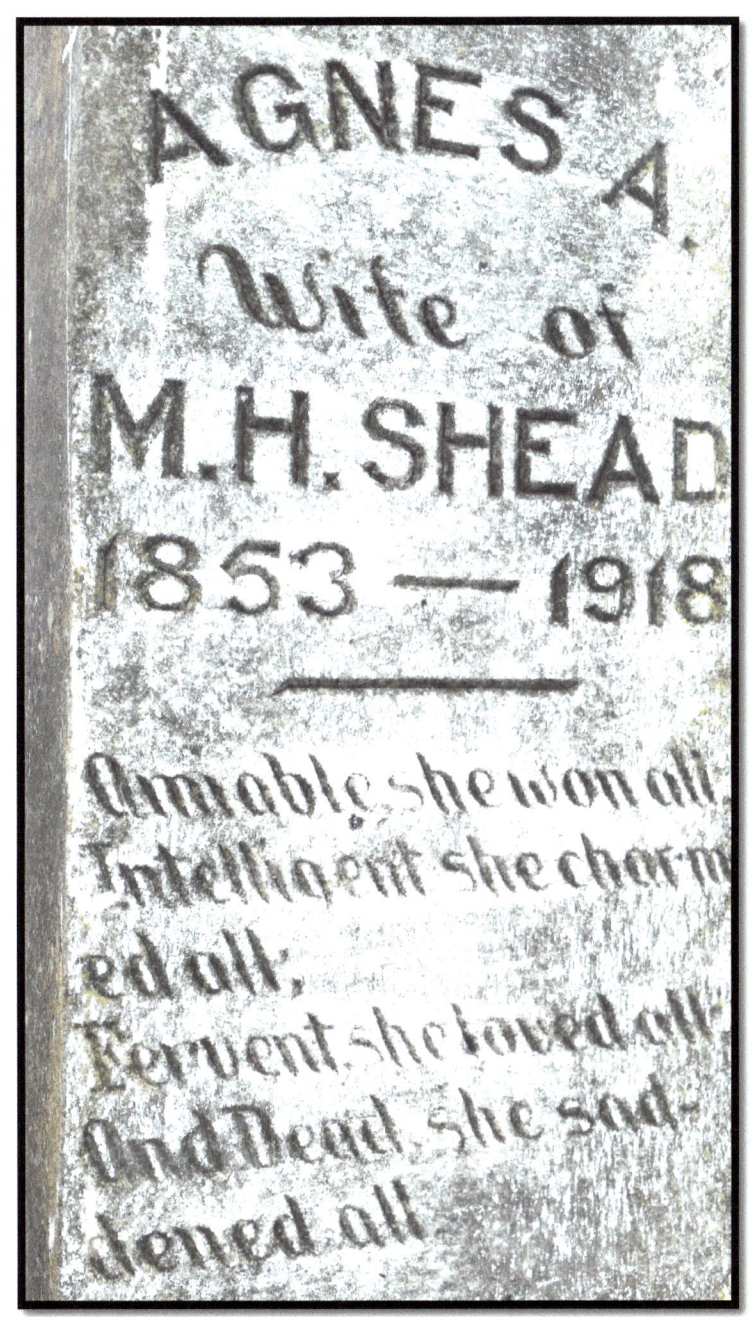

Characteristics of an 1800's Frontier Cemetery

Before Undertakers and Funeral Parlors

When the Shead Ranch Cemetery was first established, there were no professional funerary services in the region. Families prepared the departed for burial.

The body would be cleaned and dressed in the newest clothing available by the closest female relatives including wife, mother, or grandmother. After this ritual preparation, the body would be placed in the front room of the house, a parlor if the house had one, and friends would come to pay their last respects. A family member or close friend would sit up at night with the body until the day of burial, usually the next day, or at most, two.

Since church services were often conducted by circuit preachers, clergy who traveled by horse from location to location, one might not be available to conduct grave-side services. The eldest family member would read bible scripture, and custom usually called for a hymn to be sung.

Headstones were home-made and graves were excavated by relatives and friends. Coffins were constructed of whatever material was readily available. Early markers were of carved wood, and, if not replaced with something more permanent, the exact location of burial could be lost. In the ranch cemetery, several plot locations are derived from family stories and on locations of other plots.

Early professional services were costly and rare. Due to the distance of the ranch from the closest major town, Waco, professional funerary services were rarely used until around the turn of the century.

Undertakers Pucket and Littlepage had furniture stores that used the same delivery methods and construction facilities as their furniture business to make coffins. A Littlepage advertisement from the Bell Telephone directory of 1950, approximately a hundred years after the cemetery's establishment, lists both the Funeral Home and Furniture Company. Littlepage Funeral Home is still in the same location.

Ca. Late 1800s

Shepard and Ainsworth Undertakers 407 Franklin Street Waco TX

John Fall and L C Puckett Undertakers 423 Franklin Street Waco TX

J C Stephenson and Son, Undertakers 406 Austin St Waco TX

After 1900

Wilkirson and Hatch 1121 Washington Street Waco TX

Connally Funeral Home 1000 Washington Street Waco TX

Lumpkin and Dunn Undertakers, Mart TX

Littlepage Undertakers 711 East Texas Avenue Mart TX

WILKIRSON & HATCH
WASHINGTON AT 12th STREET
PHONE 63

$1.90

Name: Miss Mattie Shead
Address: Axtell, Rt. #1   Phone:
Sex: Female   Married? Single
Date of Birth: 3-17   Death: 5-1-1950
Age: 77   Waco
Hour of Death: 3:30 A.M.   Place: Home
Doctor: Nash Oliver, J.P.
Husband of (or) Wife of: Age:
Occupation: Retired
Birthplace: Shead Ranch, Texas
Father's Name: Manson Shead
Birthplace: Texas
Mother's Name: Agnes Laswell
Birthplace: Texas
Place of Burial: Shead Cemetery

100 years after the founding of the Shead Ranch

Funeral Director Book Entry for Mattie Amanda Shead, granddaughter of the ranch founder listing her place of birth as Shead Ranch, Texas.

Headstones

Upright headstones are called monuments, while headstones flat against the ground are called markers. In some modern cemeteries, only flat markers are allowed due to landscaping limitations. In the era of the Shead Ranch founding, no such restrictions are relevant. Often, the first material used to mark a grave is wood: a carved branch, planks or crossed branches. Fieldstones, chipped, painted or plain are also used.

The original markers for a grave, made by a family member in relative haste, are made with the intention of replacing them at a later date with something of permanence. If the family was moving through the area, such as in the case of infants who do not survive the harsh traveling conditions of the 1850s, it was common that a more permanent marker was never installed. It is common for frontier cemeteries to have unmarked graves.

The Shead Ranch cemetery has fieldstone markers that bear no lasting names and areas where unmarked graves are known to exist.

In Limestone County, the abundance and affordable material is the stone from which the county derives its name. This is the most prevalent marker type in the cemetery

Monument Base - Assembly Rods Missing

and also the oldest hand-fashioned type to survive to modern times. This is a rock formed by layers of sediment, vulnerable to even the mild acid in rain. Exposure to weather erodes these headstones, obscuring names and dates. The information can be displayed through raised letters or depressed letters, the latter often fairing better than the former over time.

Granite, an igneous substance formed from a molten state, is abundant to the northwest of the ranch's cemetery. Heavier and more costly than limestone, it was not in common use until the late 1800s. It is more difficult to carve than limestone.

Slate is a rare stone used in the area, porous and prone to delamination over time, but easily carved.

Marble is classed as a metamorphic rock, changing state due to heat and pressure. Marble is the most costly of the four rocks used as cemetery markers. In Shead Ranch Cemetery there are also markers made of concrete with brass engraved plaques.

Carving a stone is an art. In the earlier days of cattle ranching, a headstone could take years to be completed after the date it is requested. Early stone carvers of the region are often also furniture makers, using their carving skills and tools in both professions. Some of the markers in Shead Ranch Cemetery are made by the families of the deceased, but most that still exist were made by stone carvers based in Waco. Transportation of monuments and markers is by horse and wagon during the first years of the cemetery's use.

Pillar style monuments are constructed in pieces that are assembled on site, held together by wooden or metal rods about two inches long and inserted into small holes between the sections. Over time these rods rot or rust away. In the original construction of these monuments, cement is not used to hold pieces together. There is evidence on several monuments that restoration with cement was attempted.

Stone carving tools vary little from one stone type to the other. Patterns are traced on the stone using chalk, lead or ink. Chisels, metal tools with an angled point, make the cuts that define the edges of designs, letters and numbers. The chisel tip, an edge that varies in width from a fraction of an inch to up to two inches, is held against the drawn line and tapped on the end with a wooden mallet. The piece of stone that is broken away varies in size depending on the angle at which the chisel tip is held against the surface of the stone and the force delivered with the hammer.

To make a curved line of chipped-away stone, narrow chisel tips are used and moved in overlapping increments along the pre-drawn curve.

Rasps, most less than an inch wide, are used to remove stone within recessed designs. If the interior area to be removed is larger than an inch, grooved chisels may be used to create a textured pattern in the recessed area. Compass tools are used to ensure consistent arcs and circles.

Symbols

The design most prevalent in the Shead section of the cemetery is the equal armed cross, also called a balanced or square cross. The unusual aspect of crosses found here is the point at the end of each arm. This design does not follow the more common motif of a flared or squared end of a religious symbol.

On several of the monuments and markers of children and infants, a flying dove has been carved. Birds of any type represent eternal life or resurrection. The dove represents innocence and peace.

Lambs, curled in sleep, represent innocence and are seen on the headstones of infants and children. The lambs carved atop monuments are resting on a draped cloth, which represents mourning.

Strands of ivy are chiseled circling some of the pillar style monuments. Ivy, a perennial plant that regrows each spring, represents immortality.

Flowers represent a variety of meanings. Flowers in full bloom indicate the death occurred when the person was in the full bloom of life and are specific to women. A bud that is on a broken stem indicates the death of an infant or child, a soul that did not have an opportunity to blossom.

On the monument of James B Shead, three oval chained links are carved above his name. The links

are the symbol of the Order of Odd Fellows, a fraternal organization which focuses on charitable works. The links stand for the Odd Fellow motto, Friendship, Love and Truth, often seen on markers as F T L inside the connected ovals. The Order of the Odd Fellows originated in England in the 1700s.

Organizations of the Masons, represented by tools of a mason, an open compass and the letter G and the Eastern Star, a five-pointed star, are also fraternal associations. Both are found in Shead Ranch Cemetery.

Placement

Christian custom dictates that the side of upright monuments containing the name faces east toward the rising sun. In the ranch cemetery all but three monuments follow this custom.

The exceptions to the pattern of east facing monuments are the Watson family, a mother and two daughters and, inside the Shead Family section, a monument for the twin sons of Eugene and Claudia Thompson.

If a pillar style monument is shared, such as in the case of Fannie, wife of J M Sanderson, who was interred in 1887, one side may face east and the other another direction. Her son, Jimmie died the year before her and his side of the pillar faces east. In cemeteries near the ranch and of the same time period, some such shared pillar style monuments are set with the corner facing east so that both names are

illuminated by the rising sun. Pillar monuments shared by siblings are more commonly seen with one name above the other.

Headstones of the style known as markers, the type that lie flat are also by custom, faced toward the east.

Information

The basic information a headstone usually contains is the name of the deceased, their birth year and death year. Variations and additional information may be the full date of birth and death, name of their spouse, parent, birth location and military service. In the ranch's cemetery, the wife and daughter of the founder state the county in Tennessee where each was born. This family history was important enough to them to have made note of it chiseled in stone.

Epitaphs are statements that are placed in addition to the statistics of the deceased. Poems are often used, as are religious statements, bible quotes, terms of endearment and messages of love and loss.

The marker for Mary Elizabeth Haden has an inscription on the back, a rare placing for such information. The writing slants to the left, as is the custom for epitaphs.

"*Mother, though hast from us flown, To the regions far above. We to thee erect this stone, consecrated by our love.*"

With the uncertainty of clear rows of cemetery plots, footstones are used to denote the end of the grave. These are usually made of the same substance as the headstone, but could be simply a field stone, rounded or squared. They may be blank or contain the initials of the person interred or a relationship to the one who created the footstone such as "*Mother*" or "*Father*". Footstones professionally produced in the late 1800s of rural Texas are approximately 15 inches long, squared on all corners and designed to have about ten inches of the stone underground to help maintain an upright position. The direction of the initials, east or west, does not follow a strict pattern in the ranch cemetery. Family members who share a monument may have footstones with initials facing different directions. One footstone of note is that of Manson H Shead, with the initials facing upward.

A cenotaph is a monument placed at a location to honor the deceased, though is not the location of burial. Manson Sheid's body is not buried by the Mexican army following the taking of the Alamo and

execution of wounded prisoners. A cenotaph for him and the others who died there exists in front of the Alamo, and ashes from the pyre were gathered and are believed to be preserved in a marble coffin now displayed inside San Fernando Cathedral in San Antonio. His parents may have erected a cenotaph for him at the family homestead's cemetery in Tennessee, and if so, it does not survive there in the 21st century.

Curbing is the construction of a low concrete, brick, or metal border around a family grouping. These are common in community cemeteries of the era and locale, but none exist in Shead Ranch Cemetery as it was originally intended for only one family.

Preservation

Wrought iron fencing is a necessity in some rural cemetery locations to keep roaming cattle from toppling and breaking headstones while foraging. Shead Ranch Cemetery has one family grouping with a wrought iron barrier. The plot for J M Brown is an example of granite, with birth and death dates as well as an epitaph: "*Not dead but sleeping.*"

The Brown's wrought iron fence surrounds two plots, but only one is used. The fence, erected after 1906, would come from an ironworks shop in Waco, eighteen miles to the west. At the time, automotive vehicles of any type are a rarity, and transportation of such fencing is by horse-drawn wagon.

After 1900, chain link fences begin to replace wrought iron, due to having a more affordable cost. Shead Ranch Cemetery has two family groupings inside such fencing. These were installed around 1950.

The outer boundary of the cemetery is fenced with barbed wire on three sides and open to Limestone County Road 31 on the fourth, its southern border. The three exterior sides of pastureland protected by barbed wire are still used for cattle grazing and the fences are maintained by ranchers. Efforts have been made to fence the remaining open side of the cemetery but have not been completed to date.

A cemetery connected to a church is usually maintained by the congregation. Community cemeteries, such as the one in Mount Calm are initially maintained by family members. In later years, cemetery associations began to form in these frontier areas. Funds are established that can be drawn from for lawn care, brush removal, and mowing. The services are called perpetual care, and all modern cemeteries have such upkeep established. The cost is included in the fee paid for the burial site.

In a non-perpetual care cemetery in frontier Texas, families plant rose buses, evergreen trees and blooming bulb plants, such as irises. No restrictions or rules existed.

For private family and community cemeteries, family custom in Texas in the 1800s and later is to perform a cleaning at least once a year to remove underbrush and to specifically clear away grass burrs. The family members would bring pruning tools, hoes, shovels, rakes and brooms. The debris that is removed would be bagged and taken away as the cemeteries do not have a disposal site. During these visits, families would evaluate needed headstone repairs and perform them when possible.

SHEAD FAMILY PROFILES

SHEAD SHEID HENRY MORGAN ROBISON SANDERSON GROUP

SHEAD

The generation of Shead family members that move to Texas begins with the Ranch founder, William Robertson Shead. Born in South Carolina on April 8, 1807, he is the second of six children that survive to adulthood. He has an interest in the law and marries Amanda A Graham of Maury County, Tennessee. Amanda will remain on the extensive Sheid holdings in Tennessee, while William travels to the Mexican territory of Texas with his brother, Manson.

William is not there long before a revolt breaks out. He has been residing in Liberty, the central location of three American lawyers that will later rise in Texas politics. He rides from Liberty to Bexar in

December of 1835 to support the rebellion. His brother, Manson dies three months later.

After William's time in Bexar, he leaves the young Republic of Texas, returns alone to Tennessee, and his wife and children. He lives on the family land in Coffee County until 1850.

William and Amanda begin a permanent migration to the territory that is now part of the United States of America. Their journey, along with William's cousin, James Austin Shed, and his extensive family will take them through Arkansas and then south along the western side of the Sabine River to Shelby County, Texas.

William continues west and establishes the ranch and the cemetery, straddling Limestone and McLennan Counties. During his time there, he establishes a post office, works as a McLennan County road commissioner, a comptroller, and serves as a grand juror. He is seventy-eight when he dies in 1885. His burial location is central in the Shead section of the cemetery.

Margaret M Shead is born in Coffee County, Tennessee to William and Amanda. She travels to Texas with her family. She dies May 3, 1852 at age 15 and is purported to be the first person interred in the ranch cemetery. Though she appears on no census by name but just by number, her brother, Manson H. Shead lists her in his autobiographical sketch of Limestone County families.

Her marker, which was most likely constructed of wood, is not located on any cemetery survey in the twentieth century. The estimated location is to the north of where her mother is interred, as there is no headstone at that plot. Manson was approximately two years old when Margaret died, and was only able to relay that she was fifteen, but the month and day of death is the same

as his mother's birthdate and would have been easily remembered by a child.

Amanda M Graham Shead is born in Maury County, Tennessee. This county is west of Coffee County, home of the Sheid family. Coffee is formed in 1836, and Maury in 1807, just four years after Amanda is born. She has eleven children that survive to teens or adulthood.

Amanda precedes her husband in death in 1871. Her monument states that she was born in Maury County, Tennessee and that she is the wife of W R Shead. Her monument was obscured and displace for decades and as a result shows very little wear. A temporary marker was placed at her plot to ensure identification until restoration is complete. Her epitaph reads,

"She is not dead but sleepeth, She died as she lived, trusting in God."

The eldest son of William and Amanda, James B Shead, born in 1832, shares his father's interest in the law and serves as a McLennan County road commissioner as well as a grand juror. He runs the family cattle business until his sudden death in 1882 in East Waco at a fellow rancher's home. His wife, Esther Richards Shead arranges for a crypt in the same style as the couple had constructed for their two young daughters, Effie Shead, who died in infancy in 1867, and Virginia Shead, who died in 1874 at age 13. These three low structures are the only crypts in the cemetery. The crypts are constructed of a combination of concrete, limestone and marble. The corner blocks are concrete, with side panels being of limestone with white marble inserts.

The cover stone is limestone and each has an upright monument-style headstone displaying names and dates.

Due to the brittle nature of limestone, the monuments have been laid flat on the cover stones and positioned to face east.

Many years after the death of her husband, Esther's two remaining daughters, Caledonia Shead Morgan and Mary Ann Shead Wiley will take their mother north to Donley County near Amarillo.

Manson H Shead is born in 1850 during the family's move from Tennessee to Texas. In 1872, he marries Agnes A Lasswell, who is born in the same year as her husband. Manson works the ranch and, in later years, sells portions of it to other ranchers as well as to farmers who begin to arrive from the east around the turn of the century.

Manson and Agnes bury two of their children just north of the ranch founder, their grandfather. These children are son, Edmond M, born June 6, 1879 and died June 22, 1880, and daughter, Fannie L, born August 12, 1886 and died March 21, 1889. These children share a monument and each have a footstone bearing their initials. The monument has a sleeping lamb atop it.

Agnes Lasswell Shead dies in 1918, and Manson has a six foot tall white pillar-style monument constructed to mark her burial site. When he dies in 1923, he will have a matching pillar as his monument. These are the two most prominent monuments in the cemetery. They are easily visible in aerial photographs. Manson's footstone is of the rare style with initials facing up instead of east or west.

Mattie Amanda Shead is the eldest daughter of Manson and Agnes. She is born in 1873. She is the last family member to own parts of the ranch that surround the cemetery. Her youngest sister is Katheryn McCall Shead.

Katheryn marries Garland Johnson in 1910 and they have one child that dies in infancy. This great grandchild of the founder is buried just west of Amanda Shead. The inscription reads *Son of G D and Katie Johnson*. Shortly after, Katheryn divorces Garland and returns to using her maiden name. She and her sister, Mattie, move to Waco and run a dress shop. Katheryn goes to college and moves to St. Louis.

When Mattie dies in 1950, Katheryn returns to the ranch and has a marble monument made for her sister as well as a pre-need monument for herself. It is unknown if Katheryn was buried on the Shead ranch in 1990, or if this monument is a cenotaph, but her wishes were clear. She wanted to be beside her sister and her child.

CHILDREN OF J M SHEID, SHEID MCKINNEY Siblings

James Manson Sheid Junior, the brother of ranch founder, William, is given a quarter interest in the Limestone side of the ranch as he is also recognized as an heir to Manson Sheid who died at the Alamo. He visits the ranch on several occasions but does not establish a permanent residence there. He spends the majority of his life in Calhoun, Alabama where his wife's family have a large home. His daughter, Jane J Sheid, marries John W McKinney in Calhoun in 1875.

Shortly after their marriage, the young couple move to Limestone and reside in Mount Calm.

John sells produce, eventually opening a dry goods store and shipping produce to Waco. John is also a Mason. Jane and he have one son that survives to adulthood.

Jane Sheid McKinney dies in 1895. John erects a large three piece granite monument with her name and lists an infant on the same headstone.

John continues to live in the area with his son, James Robert McKinney. It is estimated that John W is buried ca. 1910 in the plot on the south side of his wife and infant. His marker has not been found on any survey and may have been wood or a temporary field stone marker, though large chips of a granite marker are scattered near Jane's. The next generation of this line begins to use the Prairie Hill cemetery after 1940.

James Sheid's only son, Jane Sheid McKinney's brother, Julius C Sheid also moves to Mount Calm after the 1870 census. His second child, Nannie K Sheid, born October 8, 1876 and died October 10, 1877, is interred near her aunt, Jane. This is the only existing headstone to bear the spelling of **Sheid**. Nannie's monument has the characteristic sleeping lamb seen on children's markers and monuments throughout the Shead Ranch cemetery and surrounding cemeteries. On this monument, the

lamb is curled in a protective arch. Lambs are also seen curled against a log, resting their heads. They are often atop the monument.

SHED

James Austin Shed, William's cousin who also brought his family to Texas on that journey in 1850 has no known marker. On the 1870 census, his widow, Jenny, and children, have relocated to a small community just north of the Shead Ranch's Hill County section. The census-taker records her name as Jenny Shead. It is unclear if James Austin is interred in the Shead Ranch Cemetery. It is one of three possible locations that the family has researched over the decades, with no definitive answer. His grave may be among those unmarked north of his cousin, William.

SANDERSON

Nancy Matilda Shead Sanderson (1831-1900) is the eldest daughter of the Shead Ranch founder. She comes from Coffee County, Tennessee on the move through the homestead of Seaborn Shedd (1807-1900) in Arkansas. There, she meets her future husband Morris J Sanderson. On the 1850 US Federal census, Morris is single, 21 years old, and living at home with his parents. Morris marries Nancy, and the two travel to Texas with her parents.

Nancy and Morris live on the Shead Ranch and begin a family with the birth of Edward W in 1852. Shortly after his birth, the Sandersons relocate to Bossier, LA for a few years. They remain there for the birth of William in 1854, James in 1856 and Joseph in 1857. The family is counted on the 1860 US Federal Census, Louisiana Bossier Ward 5, page one. By the 1870 census they've returned to Texas and are living on the part of the ranch that appears on the McLennan census at times, and the Limestone census some years. With them are sons Edward, William, James, and Joseph. Through the 1900 census they are consistently on Shead ranchland next to parents Nancy Matilda and Morris J. Sanderson.

In 1880, William B. Sanderson, their second son, marries S. J. who is from Florida, and their family is recorded in the 1900 census as living on the Limestone County side of the ranch. The children at home are Nannie, Clara, Raymond, and Morris.

On October 2, 1881, the third son of Morris and Nancy, James Morris Sanderson, marries Fannie Laswell (1862-1887), who is related to Nancy's sister-in-law, Agnes Laswell Shead. James and Fanny have two sons. The second, infant Jimmie Sanderson (1885-1886), is interred in the Shead Ranch Cemetery and a year later his mother Fannie Laswell Sanderson is laid to rest with him with a shared monument. His name is on the east facing part of the monument and hers on the north. Widower James Morris marries Carrie in 1891 and they are living on the Limestone side of the ranch on the 1900 census with four daughters.

The fourth son of Morris and Nancy, Joseph Sanderson, is at home with his parents in 1880, working on the Shead Ranch.

Morris buries Nancy Matilda Shead Sanderson in the Shead Ranch Cemetery in 1900, near her grandchild and daughter-in-law. The location is next to her father, the ranch founder. Her monument bears the inscription *"Born in Coffee County, Tennessee, Wife of M. J. Sanderson."* Her epithet reads,

"Rest, Mother, rest in quiet sleep, While friends in sorrow o'er thee weep."

On the 1910 US Federal Census, Morris is a widower, age 81 living in Limestone by his children and grandchildren. In 1918 Morris Joseph Sanderson is interred beside his wife. His marker of limestone is broken down to the base and the upper portion missing by the 1970 survey, the location being along a wildlife trail. Record of his interment is in the Fall and Puckett Funeral home books. His monument was located in 2014.

The family stays close to the ranch, with William R Sanderson recorded as postmaster of Watt Post Office in 1898. Watt is located one mile south of the cemetery on the border of the central portion of the ranch.

William was the third postmaster in the family, the first being William Robertson Shead, who established a post office named AMANDA on the ranch in 1857, and was followed by his son, Manson H Shead in 1891 who renamed the post office, Shead. With the exception of Morris' interment in 1918, the Sanderson family begins using the cemeteries of Mount Antioch after 1900.

HENRY

William R and Amanda M's daughter, Mary Ann Shead, is born in Tennessee. She meets Joel G Henry in Rutherford County. Joel is born in Tennessee in 1824, and his parents are both natives of Virginia, the starting point of the American Shed family. Mary Ann and Joel marry and move to the ranch by 1856. In 1863 Mary Ann and Joel bury a daughter appearing on no census, Joann Virginia Henry (1861-1863) in the Shead Ranch Cemetery. In 1868, they bury daughter, Celesta Amanda Henry (1856-1868) by her sister.

On the 1870 US Federal Census, District 48 West Texas, in their house is Laura, born 1860, William 1863, John G. 1866, and Charley 1869. They bury a third child in 1878, James Madison Henry. He does not appear on any census. These three monuments are all of the same style and are in a row from north to south in this order: Joann, Celista and then James. The age of these three monuments appears to be the same, indicating they replaced what was originally used to mark the plots. The monuments are directly east of their maternal grandparents, William R and Amanda Shead. Joann's monument has a dove of peace recessed in a circle above her name. James Madison has a lamb curled at rest above his name. Celista Amanda, named after her grandmother, has an open bible above her name.

Mary Ann and Joel C will leave the Shead ranch and move into Mount Calm, Limestone County. On the 1880 census, the family is in Mount Calm and daughter Laura has married Benjamin W. Pitts, whose extensive family moved there from Georgia.

By 1900, Mary Ann, Joel, their son John G, and Laura and Ben Pitts have left Texas and have settled in sunny San Bernardino, California. This census asks for number of children born, and number still living. She reports eight born, five living, which accounts for the three children interred in the Shead Ranch Cemetery. Their son, John G. Henry, reports he married California-born Della in 1890, which confirms that the family arrived in San Bernardino before that almost un-trackable year of the destroyed 1890 US Federal census. John G. is recorded on the census as an orange grower. The census taker records that they live on Henry Street.

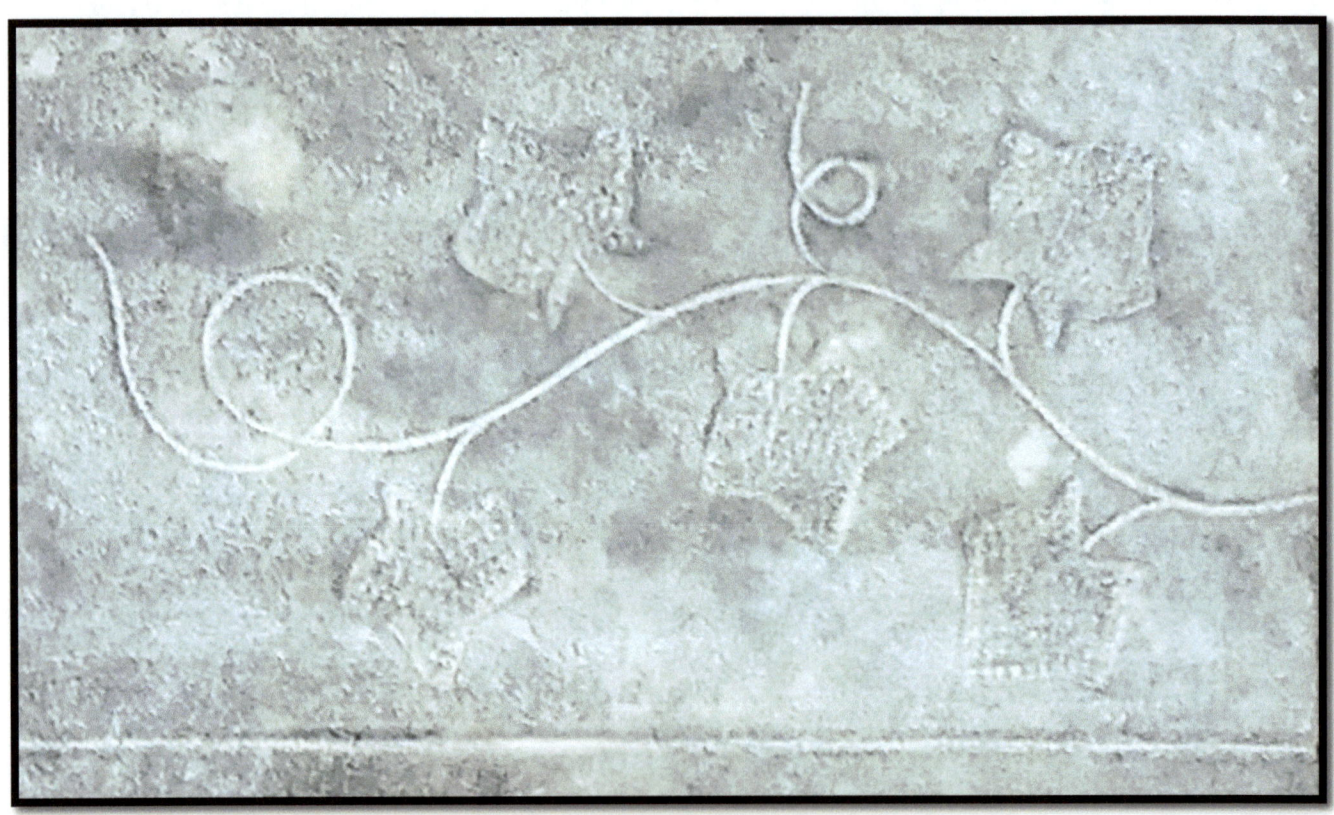

THOMPSON

Charlie and John Thompson, twin sons of Eugene A Thompson and Claudia V Morgan Thompson, are the only members of their immediate family interred in the Cemetery. The Thompson infants are buried east of their maternal great-grandfather James B's crypt. Their double monument is limestone and has the singular distinction among the Shead family of facing west. This placement may have been in error as the plot row indicates they are interred to the  east of this double monument. This monument has survived the shift of soil that has broken or buried other monuments, however it has been partially underground or covered in vegetation for many decades, resulting in a stone that is almost illegible.

Their parents left the Shead Ranch soon after 1896. There is a tie between them and the Shead family that comes to light in the far north of the Texas panhandle region. Odd Fellow cemetery, Donly County is the place where the twins' parents, E A and Claudia are buried. Odd Fellow is also where Caledonia Shead and William C. Morgan's son, James Shead Morgan is interred. Claudia Virginia Morgan in that cemetery is also a Shead descendant. Tracing that family back to the Shead ranch we find the origin of the twins. Ranch founder William's eldest son, James B Shead, had two daughters that survived to adulthood and they are Caledonia and Mary Ann. Caledonia's daughter, Claudia V Morgan, marries Eugene A Thompson on the ranch in 1895. When the couple relocate to the Texas panhandle, they have two girls: Sarah and Lillie.

In the Shead Ranch Cemetery, the monument for James B Shead bears the three interconnecting rings, symbol of the Odd Fellow Society.

LYON WALKER WOOD

Samuel H. Walker, born 1817 brings his family from Rutherford Tennessee to Texas and settles near the Shead Ranch by 1890. With him are his daughters, Maggie and Ada Belle, and son, Elihu B Walker.

James Robert McKinney
Son of Jane Sheid and John W McKinney

Thomas Obediah Wood, born 1848, brings his wife Martha Wood and family from Rutherford, Tennessee to Texas and settles in the Limestone area around 1890. They have a daughter, Alice Letha Wood.

These two Rutherford, Tennessee families may have traveled with the Henry family from the same county. Their connection to the Shead family and settlement location indicates a Tennessee connection already existed.

In 1890 the Walker and Wood families are joined when Thomas and Martha Wood's daughter, Alice Letha Wood, marries Elihu B Walker near the Shead Ranch in Limestone. They are on the 1900 census for Prairie Hill and surrounding land, which includes a thousand acres of the Limestone side of the central ranch as well as about three hundred acres north of Prairie Hill in what will later be the church and tiny settlement of Mount Antioch. In 1881, Elihu and Alice Wood Walker have Nezzie Burns Walker.

In 1902, the Walker and Wood families are joined with the Sheid family when Nezzie marries James Robert McKinney, the son of John W McKinney and Jane. J Sheid McKinney.

In 1926, Elihu B and Alice Walker bury their son, John A. Walker in the ranch cemetery. After farming for many years near the Shead Ranch, Elihu Walker is interred in the Shead Ranch

Cemetery in 1938. Martha Walker lives close by with her children until her death in 1954. She and her husband, Elihu, share a marble monument, the closest one to the county road and the southern border of the cemetery.

Thomas Obediah and Martha Wood's daughter, Ada Belle Wood, marries Thomas Wesley Lyon. Ada Belle and Thomas Wesley bury two of their children in the Shead Ranch Cemetery: Lula M Lyon in 1897 and Johnny A Lyon in 1898. The double monument is near that of Elihu B and Alice Walker.

Martha Wood is interred in 1925, and her husband, Obediah in 1927. Their son, John A Wood, is interred in 1928. All monuments are of a similar time period and located near the north end of the cemetery.

ROBISON

The Ranch founder's mother is Sibbel Robertson, with variations of the spelling of her last name on all documents that survive. Descended from her line is the Robison family. Louis and Blanche Robison ranched most likely on a portion that is within the county of Limestone. While living on the Shead ranch, they have Anna in 1870, Pinkney Thomas in 1873, Joseph in 1878, and Carroll in 1881. Daughter Anna L. Robison is interred in the Shead Ranch Cemetery in 1876, and infant Caroll B. Robison is interred in 1881.

The father of the family, Louis B. Robison, is buried there in 1884. Louis was a Mason, and his monument displays the Masonic symbol.

Pinkney Thomas Robison works at cattle ranching in Limestone until he is thirty years of age and then relocates to Terrell County. The township of Frosa on the 1900 US Federal census: Frosa is located 14 miles northwest of Grosebeck, which would place it very near where Prairie Hill is in 2013. The 1900 census reporting for the township of Frosa shows 22 year old Joseph is already a widower. He's sharing a house with his brother, Pinkney, and his mother, Blanche. His birth year would be 1878. Joseph's WW1 draft card shows he is born February 6, in 1888, has moved to Waco and his full name is Joseph Bledsoe Robison. He is married and working as a carpenter. The 1920 census again confirms his birth year as 1878. Joseph's draft card is wrong by ten years.

Blanche Locke Robison is listed on the 1900 census in Frosa township of Limestone, living with son, Pinkney. She is in the 1909 San Angelo city directory as a widow, and her late husband's name is listed as Louis B. She is living with her son, Joseph, at this time. After Louis died in 1884, she had arrangements to be buried back in the Shead Ranch Cemetery with her husband and two of her children, infant Carrol B and Anna, and is interred in July 1928. A chain link fence with a south facing gate surrounds Blanche and Louis' monuments. His is of limestone, and hers of marble. Carroll B and Anna's monuments are just north of the fence and are of marble approximately the same date of making as Blanche's, the originals having been replaced. Footstones remain at these plots, made of limestone. After her death, Joseph and his wife will return to the area around the ranch. He lives until age 78 and is interred in the Prairie Hill Cemetery where many ranch residents of later years are interred.

AREA FAMILY PROFILES

The following listings have no clear family connection to the ranch founder's family. Most worked within the original borders of the ranch, and some were life-long friends of William and Amanda and their children, grandchildren and great-grandchildren. The groupings are arranged alphabetically.

A through G

ARNOLD BUCHANAN DONOHO SMITH OLIVER FAMILY

In 1838 in the Republic of Texas, Mortimer Donoho has arrived from Tennessee to try his hand at frontier cattle raising. He marries Easter Baker and the two settle east of Waco, within ten miles of where

William Shead will later establish his ranch. The Donohos begin their family with Archie, born in 1836.

Their fourth son, Austin Donoho is born in Texas in 1850, the year before the Shead family return to settle permanently in Texas. On the 1860 census for McLennan, Austin's father Mortimer Donoho is listed as a stock raiser. His mother is listed as E. B. Donoho, and Mortimer has four brothers. The D. C. Vaughn family lives with them and will be identified on a later census as cousins. D. C. also came from Tennessee. Recorded by the 1860 census taker, Mr. Donoho has a sprawling ranch with a sizeable herd worth $10,250. The Vaughn family also have cattle worth $2370. Stock raiser and the earlier term for cowboy, stock tender, is recorded as occupations for the adult men of the family.

Austin grows up working as a cowboy on the eastern edge of McLennan County and meets the Malone family, nearby neighbors.

The Malone family comes to Texas from Tennessee by way of Louisiana, arriving in the 1860s. They farm east of Waco. Alpha is the eldest of two daughters and she has three brothers. She marries William Buchanan around 1875, and they have two sons before William's early death in 1878.

Austin Donoho and Alpha marry in 1879 and name their first son after Austin's brother, Archie. They have William in 1887 and Annie in 1890. Austin dies the year following the birth of his daughter. He is the first of this family to be interred in the Shead Ranch Cemetery in 1891. Alpha, now twice widowed and with five children, marries William Smith nine years after Austin's death. She lives with Mr. Smith in Waco until his death.

John William Alexander of Tennessee also brings his family to Texas. In the household are daughters Ida and Mattie.

Alpha's second son, William Middleton Buchanan Jr, marries Ida Cornelia Alexander in 1897, and they are back living on the Shead Ranch. William is a blacksmith and also farms. A year into their marriage they have a daughter, W. E. Buchanan, and when she dies in 1898, William and Ida bury her on her grandfather Austin's right side, in the Shead Ranch Cemetery. The monument reads, "*Dau. Of W. M. & I. C. Buchanan*", with a footstone bearing her initials, *W. E. B.*

Willie C Arnold, age 7, is interred in 1899. The monument bears only initials, but his first name is found in the details that remain from Waco funeral home records as follows: Arnold, Willie 8 yrs; by Jim Kellum, for Jno. Arnold; d. Dec. 25, 1899; interred at Elk, Dec. 26; casket 17.00; Book 17 of the Fall and Puckett series, page 4668, a collection of various undertakers. Willie is the grandchild of John W Alexander, and the son of Ida Buchanan's sister, Mattie and her husband, John G Arnold. On the 1900 US Federal census for Limestone County, the Prairie Hill and Mount Antioch district 0054, sheet 21, the

Arnold family is listed in the household of J Alexander, a 62 year old widower. All family members are born in Tennessee. The family has J's son, J P, age 33, James B Alexander, age 19, and the Arnolds. Mattie Arnold is J Alexander's daughter, age 28, and her husband John Arnold is age 30. Mattie reports she's

had two children, one still alive. That living child is Maggie, born in 1897, and her birth state shows that the family is in Tennessee in 1897. Just four houses away is the family of J W McKinney, the recent widower of Jane J Sheid McKinney. C T Sheid, born in Texas in 1879, has just married Lizzie, and the young couple are living with the McKinney family. Mattie and John return to Tennessee before the 1910 census. They will have another child who they also name Willie.

Hassie Earl Oliver is born in 1907 and, a year later, is interred in the Shead Ranch Cemetery. Hassie is the child of Austin and Alpha Donoho's daughter, Annie, and her husband, Daniel E Oliver.

William and Ida Buchanan leave Texas for a short time, working in Oklahoma, but return to their former home after two years. In 1910, they bury a son, Luther Buchanan in Shead Ranch Cemetery. His limestone monument reads, "*Son of W. M. & Ida Buchanan.*"

In 1931, Alpha passes away at the home of her son just a few miles from the Shead Ranch. William and Ida bury her by Austin and her two grandchildren. Her marker is an engraved bronze plaque set in concrete faced with tiny round pebbles. Austin's original marker is replaced with one matching Alpha's.

William and Ida raise two more children to adulthood and remain in the gentle rolling land around the Shead Ranch for the remainder of their lives. William and Ida share a monument in the ranch cemetery near Alpha and their two children, William being interred in 1944, and Ida in 1951. The inscriptions are "*Father*" and "*Mother*".

This family group stays closely associated with the Shead family. Archie Donoho is listed as one of the pall bearers for the last member of the Shead family to live on the ranch, Mattie Amanda Shead.

AUBERRY BRADBURY EARLS HUGHES CATES FAMILY GROUP

Adeline Hughes is born in 1832 in Tennessee, and comes to Texas with her daughter, Mickey Earls, born 1859, and grandson, Elias J Earls, born 1879. Mickey's daughter Nannie Belle Auberry marries George Allen.

Auberry, George Allen, is a land owner and employer on the 1940 US Census. On the Texas Death index we find him listed as residing in Limestone on 1-28-1945.

Nannie and George's daughter, Mattie Lee Bradbury, is buried with two infants in 1940.

The 1977 survey lists Hand, Bill A. On the 1940 census Limestone precinct 2 home of the Auberry family, daughter Willie and husband Raymond Hand are visiting from McLennan County, Willie "Bill" Myrtle Hand dies at age 92, May 13, 2000 and is buried in McLennan County. The marker observed in '77 is removed before the 2003 survey.

Claudy E Cates, born in 1892 has a marker surveyed in 1977 within this family group that shows a death year of 1894. This is the grandchild of Robert B Cates and Catherine Elizabeth Staden. Their eldest son, Robert Lee Cates, married into the Earls Doak family.

BEACON

A marker for Maria Nancy Beacon, 1918 is surveyed in 1977 but is not found during the survey in 2003. No Beacon family appears on a census for the area or on funeral home records and the '77 entry may have been a transcription error.

BERALEK

Around 1875, Jan and Marie Beralek emigrate from Austria Bohemia to Texas, along with their sons, Ludvick, Anton, and Martin. In Texas, they settle near Elk and raise another son, Joe. Jan dies in 1909 and Marie in February, 1911, they are buried beside each other in the Shead Ranch cemetery. Martin works as a farmer and he never marries. Ludvick, also a farmer, reported to the census taker in 1930 that he is divorced and that his birth place is Austria. Ludvick and his brother, Martin, are interred beside their parents almost thirty years later. Ludvick Beralek, 1870 – 1941, and Martin Beralek, February 21, 1874 to May 14, 1931, have temporary markers as supplied by Lumpkin's Funeral Home of Mart. Jan and Marie's original markers are replaced with a double monument written in Czech. There is a large Czech settlement about sixty miles west of the ranch. On all forms before 1940, the family's point of origin is Austria. Bohemia is listed as the language spoken at home on some census. It is a region that is south of Austria.

BOYKIN

Early census for the Boykin family: 1850 census R H Boykin, born in 1821 in Alabama and his first wife is Nancy, born 1826 with children Wm, Jno, Daniel, Elisabeth born 1849. 1860 census R H Boykin, William, John, Daniel, Sara born 1850, Margaret, Mary, James and Isaac born 1859. By the 1880 census R H has a new wife.

Isaac N Boykin, son of R H, is born in Mississippi in 1859 and is in Texas by age 1. He marries Ann Elizabeth Riley in 1879. Their eldest son is James Richard. In 1910, James Richard Boykin is listed on the Leon County Federal Census with his wife, May. In the household is his Aunt, Maggie Martin, born in 1854. She's been married for eighteen years, but her husband is not in the household at the time of the census. James Richard is also raising his two young cousins, Barker and Bessie, both born in Texas, in 1902 and 1903, respectively. An educated man, he owns his farm. There are several prosperous Boykin family farms in Leon County.

Around 1910, James Richard Boykin moves north to Limestone and works at farming. He is interred in the Shead Ranch Cemetery in 1915. James Richard's death certificate lists his place of burial as Shead Ranch Cemetery, which verifies his full name, marital status, and that he is living on the McLennan side of the ranch. The undertaker is Lumpkin's Funeral Home of Mart, Texas.

There was confusion about where James was buried. His family in Leon County had erected a monument for him in their family cemetery. That Leon County monument is a cenotaph. James Richard Boykin on the Texas death index; 1903-1940, page 2575, certificate 1687, Richard Boykin McLennan 1-27-15.

His child, Jessie Lee Boykin, is interred by him in 1916. The two family members have matching limestone markers side by side in the south-east corner of the cemetery. Census following the interment of Jessie Lee Boykin indicate this family abandons farming in Limestone and returns south to Leon County were others of the prosperous Boykin family reside.

BROWN

John Michael BROWN comes to Texas from Mississippi and marries Frances Angeline Braden. They raise a family in Leon County, which borders Limestone on its southern edge. Before the 1900 US Federal Census, he has moved north and has purchased land next to the home of Manson H Shead. Sons Terry,

Otto and Norman are living at home. In 1906, John Michael passes away and is interred in the Shead Ranch Cemetery.

An intricate wrought iron fence is constructed around his grave and a large monument is erected. The fence defines a second burial site, intended for his wife's use. His family continues to farm the land next to Manson H Shead's family. On the 1910 US Federal Census for McLennan County, Terry Wiley Brown is now head of house. Eleanor and Terry are raising Alpha, Norene, J. M, and Hubert C Brown. They own their home and do what the census taker determines to be "general farming". On this census, the enumeration is for the town of Axtell and Elk. The ranch borders Elk on the north and is east of Axtell. Terry will remain farming the land his father bought for many years. Fannie moves on to Taylor County with her son, Otto, and his wife, Blanche. She will not be interred next to her husband.

CALVERY and SWINNEY, the HENDERSON SISTERS

Jacob J Henderson is born in 1822 in Georgia. He moves from there to Prentiss Mississippi and raises daughters Alice E, born in 1857 and Harriet Callie, born in 1862. These sisters will move to Texas.

Harriet Callie Henderson and Doc J Calvery marry in Prentiss Mississippi. They relocate to Texas before 1890. Doc and two of his brothers, all sons of Thomas H. Calvery Jr. of Prentiss, have moved to the Shead ranch area. In 1890, Doc has buried his first wife on the Shead Ranch. Harriet Callie Calvery is twenty-eight years old when she dies on August 10, 1890. Doc will remarry in two years. In 1900, on the census that covers the Shead ranch is Mary C Smith Calvery, a widow of James Rowden Calvery, raising four children next door to R F Alexander. Looking through the area census, we find James Rowden's brother, Anderson Word Calvery, and we find Doc J Calvery with his second wife.

Harriet's sister, Alice E Henderson Swinney's monument lists her birth and death dates as November 19, 1857 – December 23, 1892. The monument identifies her as the wife of T C Swinney. Thomas Clayton and she came from Prentiss Mississippi and spent a short time living at the ranch. After her death, Thomas remarries, moves to Oklahoma for a short time and then settles in Palo Pinto, Texas.

CHRISTIAN

John Logan Christian is born in Missouri in 1870 and his parents relocate to Summit, Boone County, Arkansas. John grows up in Arkansas and in 1891, marries Sophronia Jane Swofford. They have five children in Arkansas, and their last census in that state is taken in 1900. John moves the family to McLennan County, Texas and works by the Shead ranch. Sophronia Swofford Christian dies in 1907, the year she gives birth to her only child born in Texas, Arnie. Her monument in the Shead Ranch Cemetery bears the symbol of the Eastern Star and has a sculpture of an open bible.

John moves his young family to the city of Hillsboro in Hill County and remains there through the 1920 census. John Logan's eldest son, Charles R., moves back to Summit, Arkansas and John soon follows to retire with Charles and his wife, Mary Donna Qualls, and many grandchildren.

A possible connection to the Shead family is found on the 1910 US Federal census. In 1910, the son of Manson H. Shead, Thomas R Shead, and his wife, Cordelia, are living in a boarding house in Cisco, Eastland, Texas. Also with them is Carl Swofford, born in Texas in 1881. It is not clear if Carl is a brother of Sophronia.

DAVIS

In 1831, in Roane County, Tennessee, Nathaniel Thomas Davis has arrived from Kentucky and marries Malinda Oden. They move to Blount County, Alabama for the birth of their third son, John Phineas Davis in 1836. Nathaniel reports his profession as farmer. After the 1850 US census, the Davis family, now with eight children at home, move on to Smith County, Texas. On September 18, 1856 John marries Matilda L Stephenson. She is also from Blount County, Alabama and has been in Texas since before the 1850 US census where she's listed at age 12 with her parents, W H and Elizabeth. The census lists the birth states of her siblings, showing that the Stephenson family moved from Alabama to Tennessee in 1843, residing there for the birth of twins and one other child in 1845 before coming to Texas.

By 1865, John is a widower raising two sons, Nathan and James. He then marries Macon Frances Chandler, a widow with two sons, William "Buck" and Harvey Cooper. Leon County is the seat of the family, with John joining the Masonic lodge of Centerville in Leon County in 1877 and is later a member of the Buffalo

J P Davis

lodge in the same county. On the 1880 US census. He lists his profession as farmer.

Macon and John have six more children: George, Elizabeth, John P Junior in 1872, Andrew, Allen in 1876 and a son named Warren "Doc" Chandler born in 1878.

After that 1880 census, John Phineas Davis relocates to Limestone on the eastern end of the central portion of the ranch. Due to the lost US census of 1890 it is unclear which year the family relocates to Limestone. The soil in the region is prime for growing grains and a market for produce is about twenty miles west in Waco.

In 1896, he passes away. John has a Masonic Symbol on his limestone monument. His plot has a footstone.

Macon and three of her grown sons, John P, Allen, and Warren, are living on the eastern edge of the ranch, according to the 1900 US Census. This census stretches north from Prairie Hill, across Christmas Creek beyond the eastern end of the ranch's central portion, north to Mount Antioch where Charles B Shead and Manson H Shead raise horses and grow produce.

Within ten years, she will leave Limestone and retire to Chillicothe, Texas to live with her eldest son, William "Buck" Cooper.

H through W

HADEN

Mary Elizabeth Haden, age 12 at interment in September 1985, is the daughter of W O and I R Haden. The family does not appear on any census.

JANES and MANGRUM Infants

Infant A Janes, born December 3, 1897, is interred in the cemetery in February of the following year. Record of the burial is listed in Waco's Fall and Puckett Funeral director's books, notating that it is a child of A Janes. Also in the Fall and Puckett books is Lelia Mangrum, an infant interred in the Shead Ranch Cemetery. Birth year is 1896 and interment is September 9, 1897. The location of these graves are estimated by placement of rocks and appear on no surveys. No family named Mangrum or Janes are on area census for the years surrounding 1896 or 97.

POLSON

Ethel Pearl Holiday Polson grows up in the vicinity of the ranch with her widowed mother and four siblings. At seventeen, she marries Bert Taylor Polson. Ethel has three children before she dies in childbirth in 1920. Her limestone monument bears the inscription *"Wife of Bert Taylor Polson."* An infant is listed with her.

Widower Bert marries widow Annie Early Howard and blends the families, now consisting of five children. Bert farms in the area until his retirement.

PEREZ

Manuel Perez listed on the 1977 survey. Feb 7, 1887, Sept 7, 1924. No Perez' are on area census and a marker is not located during the Jordan survey, so this may have been a transcription error.

RIVERS

Carrie Ferguson marries William Alfred Rivers in Prairie Hill in 1891. William's family comes to Texas from Mississippi when he is twelve, and they farm near the Shead ranch. Carrie Rivers died shortly after the two are wed. There is no record of any children of this marriage. Her monument has the epitaph, "*Wife of W. A. Rivers*". William remarries and remains in the Prairie Hill area until his retirement at age 70.

TILLMAN

J C Tillman, born March 8, 1835, is 49 when he passes away November 21 1894. This monument bears no inscription other than dates. Due to the destroyed US Census of 1890, the Tillman family has not been located.

WATSON

Samantha A Watson and Oliver Watson marry in Mississippi, and their first two children are born there. They relocate to Texas, settling on the eastern end of the ranch by 1882 and the birth of Felix. Their family is found on the 1900 census with O and S A as head, and children Felix, Clara, Ethel, Ollie, Amos and Eva N. Three members of the Watson family are interred in the Shead Ranch cemetery. Lelia M E Watson, born September 29, 1889, dies November 23, 1890 and Ada Pearl Watson, born April 20, 1878 in Mississippi, dies September 25, 1895. Mother, Samantha A Watson, born April 22, 1860, dies June 15, 1904 and is buried by her daughters.

Samantha A has an Eastern Star symbol on her monument. The inscription reads, "*Wife of O Watson*" and the inscription on the daughter's monuments read, "*Dau of O & S Watson*". After Samantha's passing in 1904, Oliver marries Fannie and is on the 1910 census in Limestone Precinct 2. He is widowed again by 1920, now in Mart, where he owns a home he shares with his youngest child, Eva. His occupation is cotton buyer and his children work in a retail dry goods store.

WILLIAMS

William L Williams is born in 1843 and is 82 when he passes away in 1925. He is not listed on the Texas death index or on a census. His interment is near the Walker Lyon group.

72

Maps and Headstone Locations

Known Plots. Cemetery detail maps follow.
Blue listings are Shead and related families.

Last Name	First Name	Birth	Death	Age	Chart #	Loc H	Loc V
Arnold	W C	1892	1899	7	1	C	19
Auberry	George A	1875	1945	70	2	B	20
Auberry	Nannie	1881	1959	80	3	B	20
Beralek	Jan	1844	1909	65	5	N	22
Beralek	Ludvick	1870	1941	70	76	L	22
Beralek	Marie	1838	1911	73	6	N	22
Beralek	Martin	1875	1941	65	77	L	22
Boykin	James R	1883	1915	22	7	N	22
Boykin	Jessie Lee	1914	1916	2	8	N	22
Bradbury	Mattie L	1906	1940	34	9	B	19
Brown	J M	1841	1906	55	11	L	17
Buchanan	Ida C	1879	1951	72	12	C	19
Buchanan	Luther	1902	1910	12	13	C	19
Buchanan	W E	1898	1898	0	14	E	19
Buchanan	William	1877	1944	67	15	C	19
Calvery	Harriet C	1862	1890	28	16	F	10
Cates	Claudy E	1892	1894	2	17	B	19
Christian	Sophronia	1871	1907	36	18	I	10
Davis	John P	1836	1896	60	19	M	20
Donoho	Austin	1850	1891	41	20	D	19
Earls	Elias J	1879	1944	65	22	C	20
Earls	Mickey F	1859	1936	77	24	C	20
Haden	Mary E	1888	1895	7	26	H	12
Henry	Celista Amanda	1856	1868	12	28	H	20
Henry	James Madison	1876	1878	2	29	H	20
Henry	Joann Virginia	1861	1863	2	30	H	20
Hughes	Adeline	1832	1918	76	31	C	20
Janes	A	1897	1898	1		M	22
Johnson	Infant	1911	1911	0	32	H	18
Lyon	Johnnie A	1898	1899	1	33	N	21
Lyon	Lula M	1897	1897	0	34	N	21
Mangrum	Lelia	1896	1897	1		M	22
McKinney	John J	1845	1910	65	35	J	20
McKinney	Jane J & Inf	1845	1895	50	36	J	20
Oliver	Hassie E	1907	1908	1	75	D	19
Polson	Ethel P & Inf	1897	1920	23	38	H	8

Last Name	First Name	Birth	Death	Age	Chart #	Loc H	Loc V
Rivers	Carrie	1873	1893	20	40	F	10
Robison	Anna L	1870	1876	6	41	H	22
Robison	Blanche R	1844	1928	84	43	I	21
Robison	Carrol B	1880	1881	1	42	I	21
Robison	Louis B	1827	1884	57	44	I	21
Sanderson	Fannie	1862	1887	25	45	G	18
Sanderson	Jimmie	1885	1886	1	46	G	18
Sanderson	Morris Joseph	1829	1918	89	74	I	19
Sanderson	Nancy Matilda	1831	1900	69	47	I	19
Shead	Agnes A	1853	1918	65	48	I	18
Shead	Amanda M	1811	1871	60	49	H	19
Shead	Edmond M	1879	1880	1	50	H	18
Shead	Effie	1875	1875	0	51	F	20
Shead	Fannie L	1886	1889	3	52	H	18
Shead	James B	1832	1882	49	53	E	20
Shead	Katheryn M	1892	1990		54	G	19
Shead	Manson H	1850	1923	73	55	J	18
Shead	Margaret M	1838	1852	15	76	H	19
Shead	Mattie Amanda	1874	1950	74	73	G	19
Shead	Virgina	1861	1874	13	57	F	20
Shead	William R	1807	1885	78	58	H	19
Sheid	Nannie K	1876	1877	1	56	H	21
Smith	Alpha Donoho	1855	1931	76	59	D	19
Swinney	Alice E	1857	1892	35	60	F	11
Thompson	Charlie	1895	1896	1	61	E	21
Thompson	John T	1895	1896	1	62	E	21
Tillman	J C	1835	1894	49	63	O	21
Walker	Alice Letha	1870	1954	84	64	O	23
Walker	Elihu B	1858	1938	80	65	O	23
Watson	A Pearl	1878	1895	17	66	D	10
Watson	Lelia M	1889	1890	1	67	E	10
Watson	S A	1860	1904	44	68	D	10
Williams	Wm L	1843	1925	82	69	M	22
Wood	John A	1884	1928	44	70	D	18
Wood	Martha Louise	1846	1925	79	71	D	18
Wood	Thomas O	1847	1927	80	72	D	18

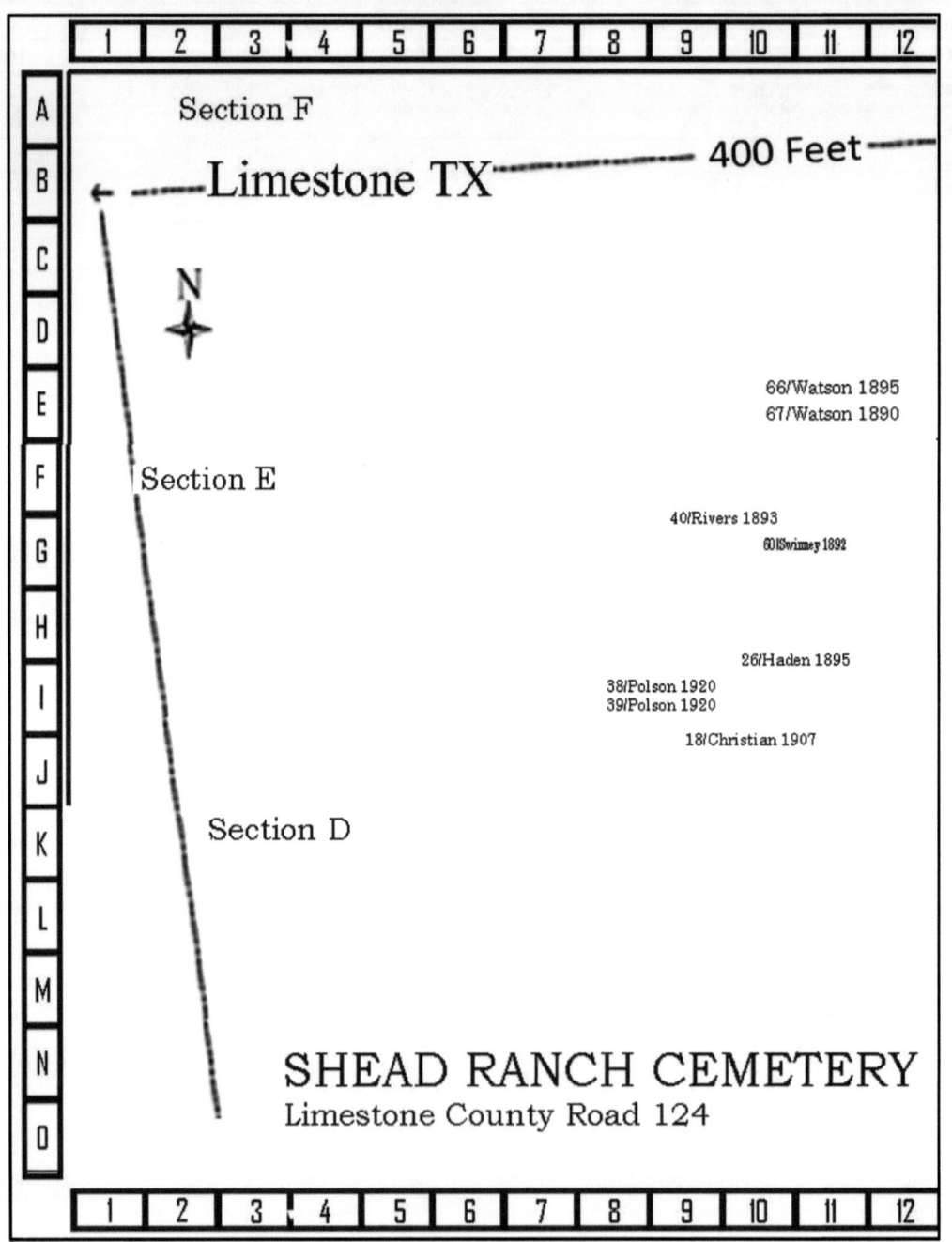

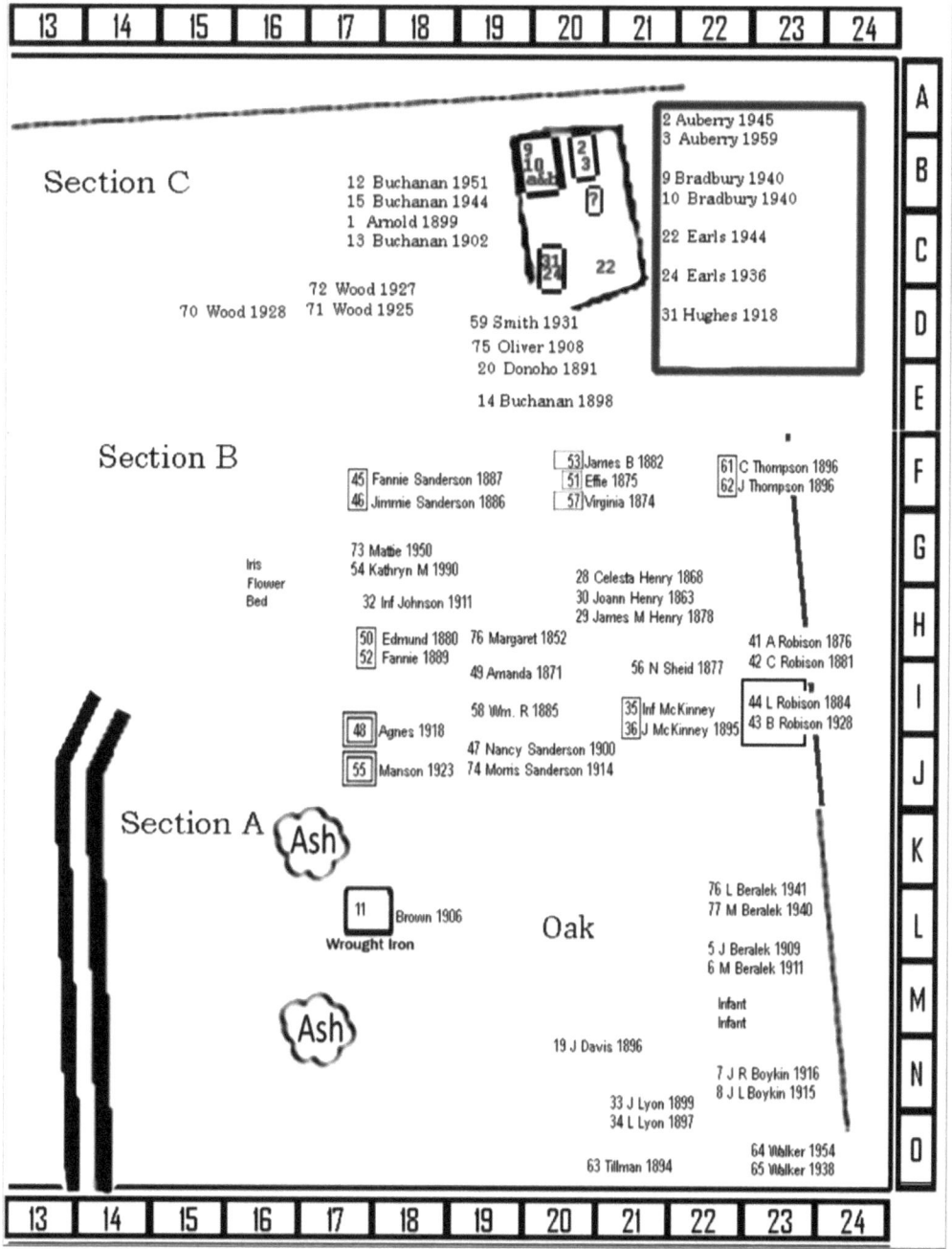

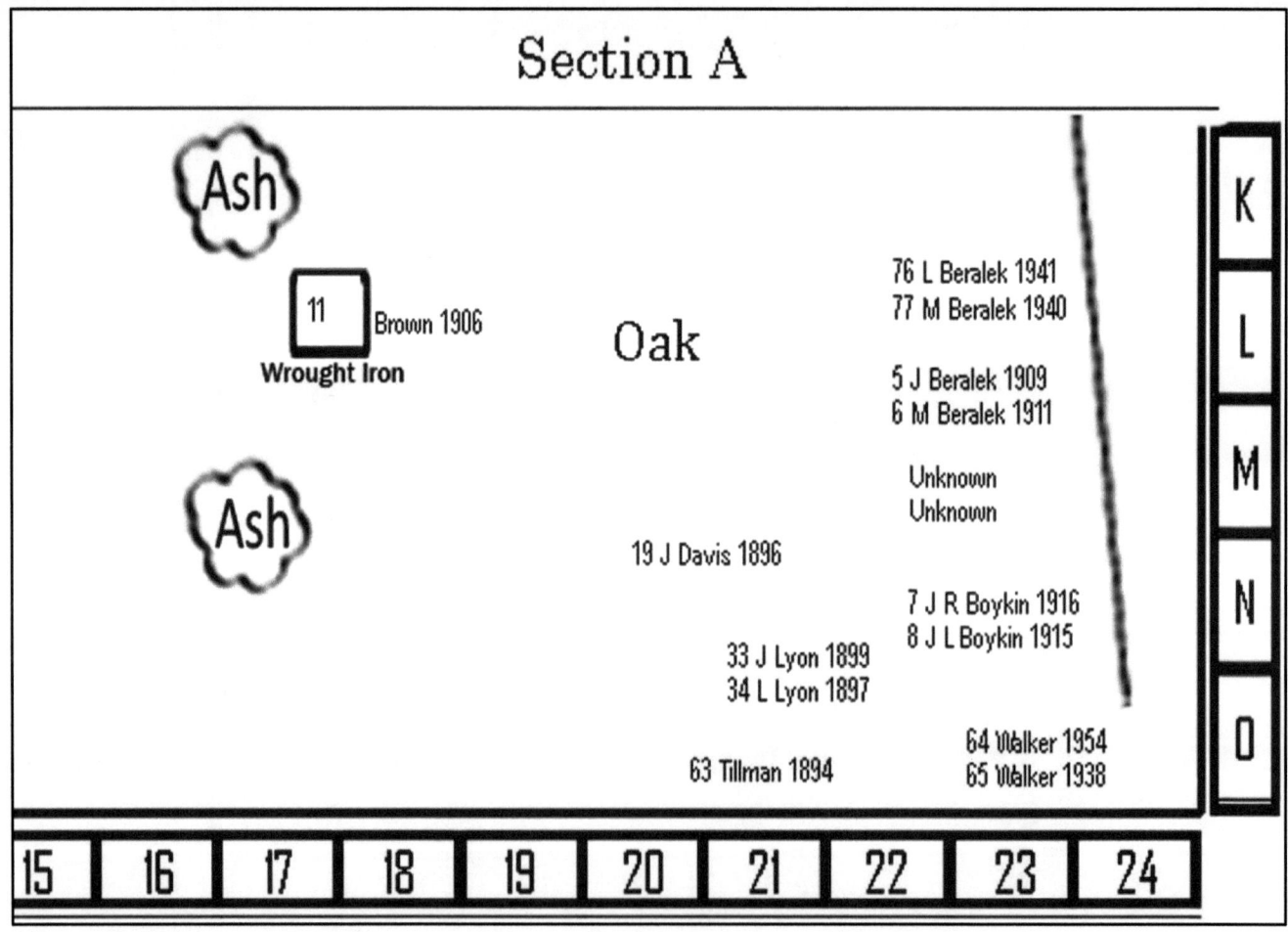

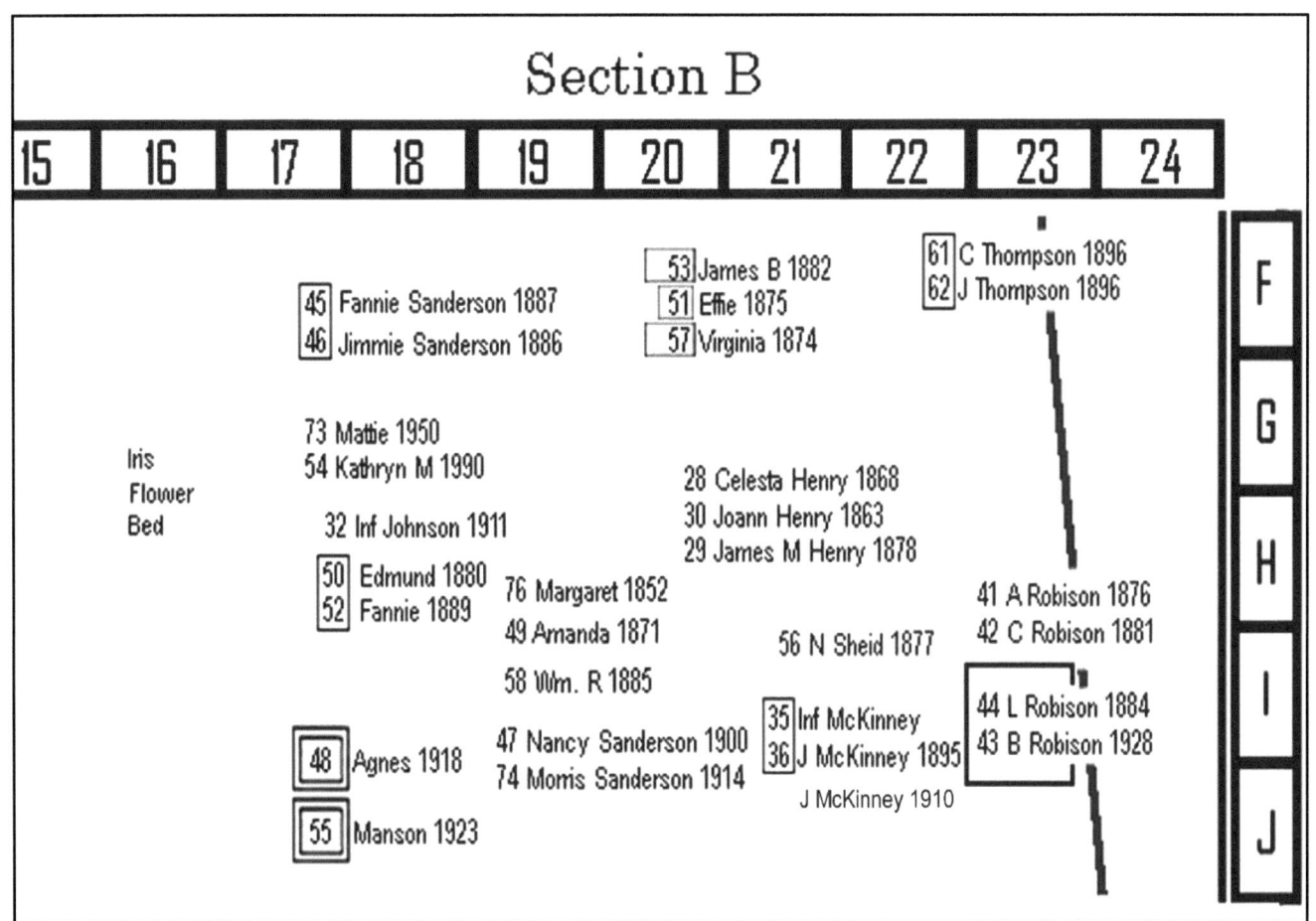

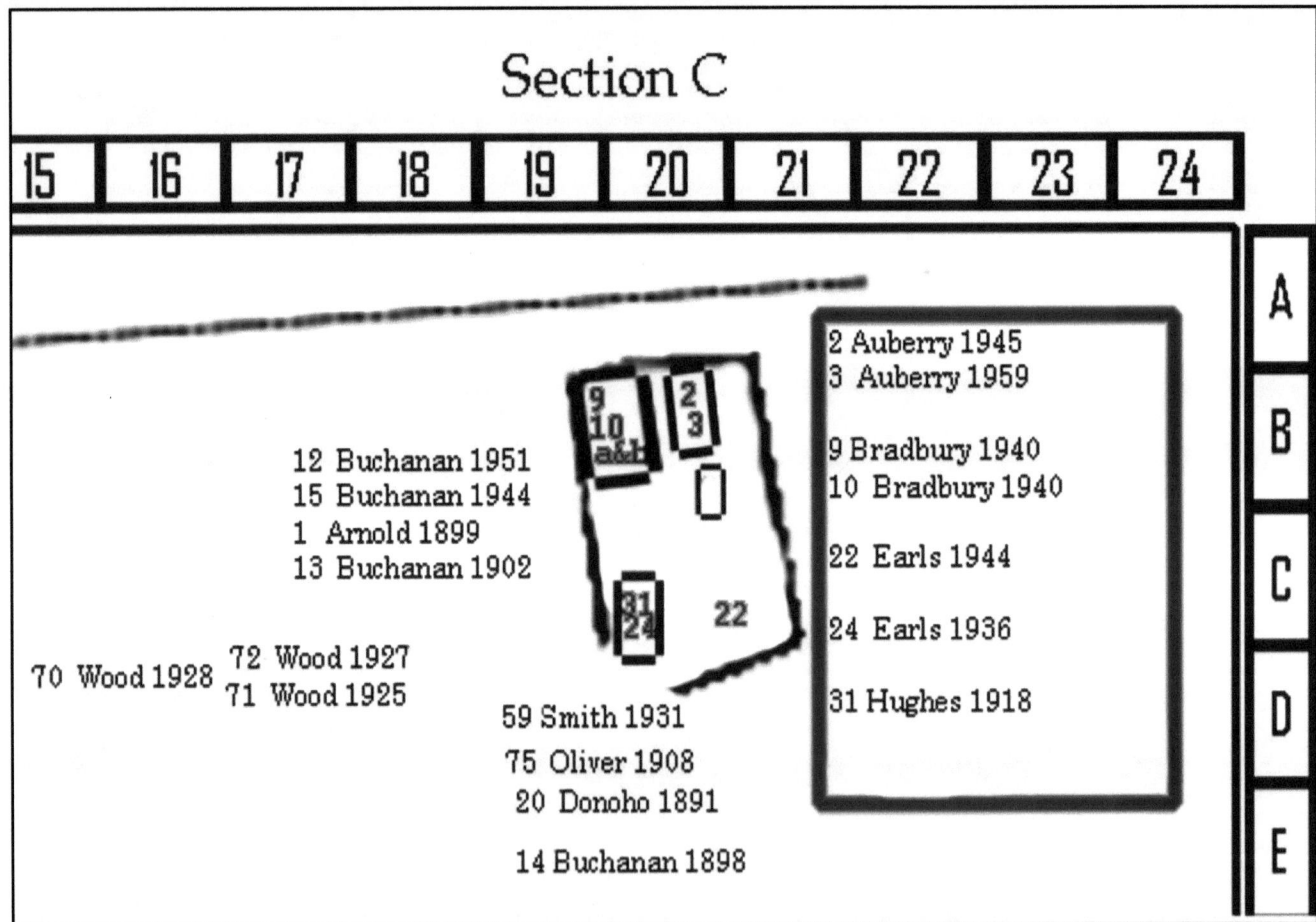

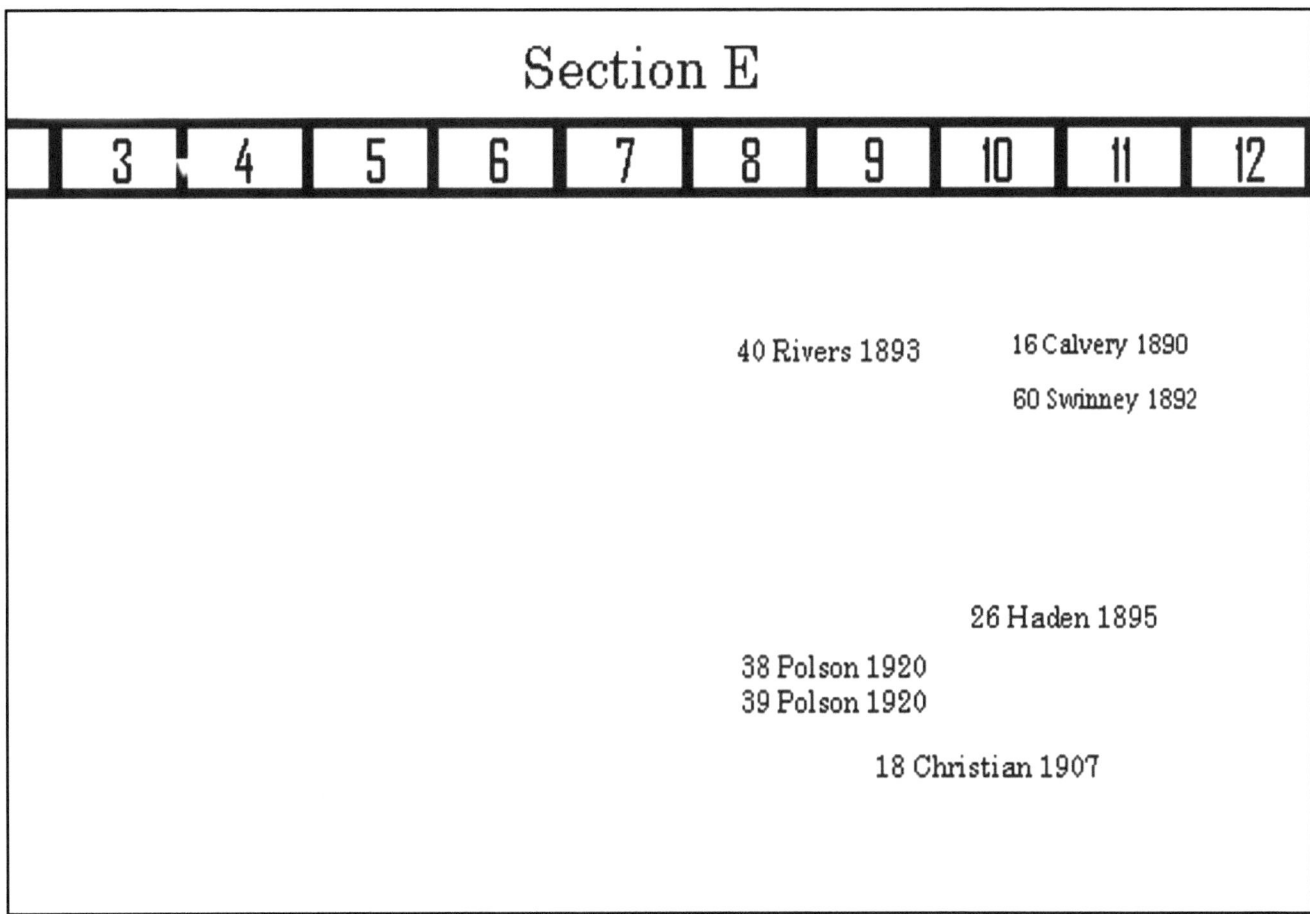

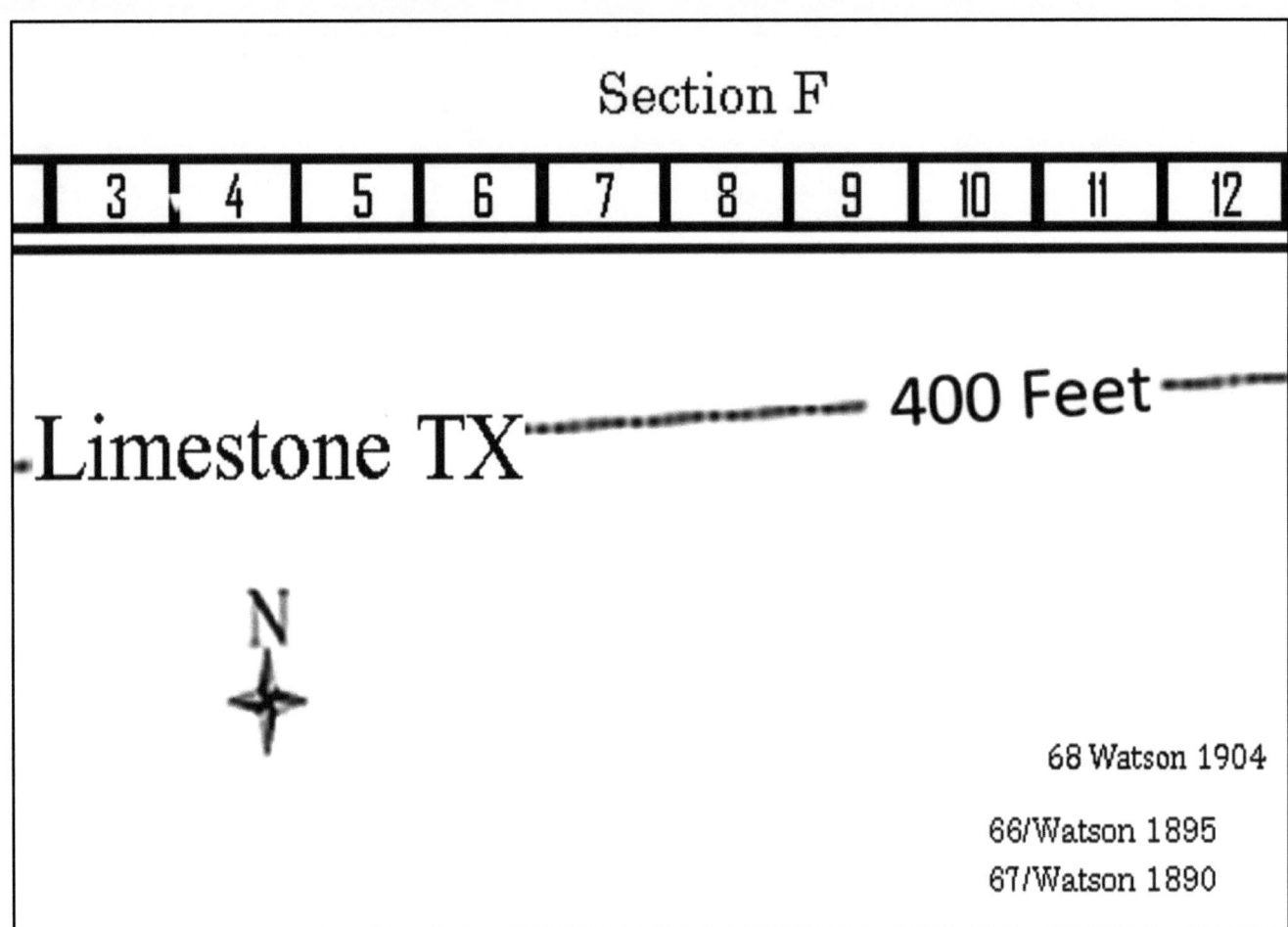

Ordered By Year of Interment

Surname	Given	Year	Surname	Given	Year
Shead	Margaret M	1852	Watson	S A	1904
Henry	Joann Virginia	1863	Brown	J M	1906
Henry	Celista Amanda	1868	Christian	Sophronia J	1907
Shead	Amanda M	1871	Oliver	Hassie Earl	1908
Shead	Virgina	1874	Beralek	Jan	1909
Shead	Effie	1875	Buchanan	Luther	1910
Robison	Anna L	1876	Beralek	Marie	1911
Sheid	Nannie K	1877	Johnson	Infant	1911
Henry	James Madison	1878	Boykin	James R	1915
Shead	Edmond M	1880	Boykin	Jessie Lee	1916
Robison	Carrol B	1881	Beacon	Maria Nancy	1918
Shead	James B	1882	Hughes	Adeline	1918
Robison	Louis B	1884	Sanderson	Morris Joseph	1918
Shead	William R	1885	Shead	Agnes A	1918
Sanderson	Jimmie	1886	Polson	Ethel Pearl	1920
Sanderson	Fannie	1887	Polson	Infant	1920
Shead	Fannie L	1889	Shead	Manson H	1923
Calvery	H C	1890	Williams	Wm L	1925
Watson	Lelia M E	1890	Wood	Martha L	1925
Donoho	Austin	1891	Wood	Thomas O	1927
Swinney	Alice E	1892	Robison	Blanche R	1928
Rivers	Carrie	1893	Wood	John A	1928
Cates	Claudy E	1894	Smith	Alpha Donoho	1931
Tillman	J C	1894	Earls	Mickey F	1936
Haden	Mary Elizabeth	1895	Walker	Elihu B	1938
McKinney	Infant	1895	Bradbury	Mattie Lee	1940
McKinney	Jane J	1895	Bradbury	Two Infants	1940
Watson	A Pearl	1895	Beralek	Ludvick	1941
Davis	John P	1896	Beralek	Martin	1941
Thompson	Charlie	1896	Buchanan	William M	1944
Thompson	John T	1896	Earls	Elias J	1944
Lyon	Lula M	1897	Auberry	George A	1945
Mangrum	Lelia	1897	Shead	Mattie A	1950
Buchanan	W E	1898	Buchanan	Ida C	1951
Janes	A	1898	Walker	Alice Letha	1954
Arnold	W C	1899	Auberry	Nannie	1959
Lyon	Johnnie A	1899	Earls	John N	1965
Sanderson	Nancy Matilda	1900	Earls	Attie M	1973

Listing by year of interment helps determine the gap in headstones made of materials that do not last and those viewable today. Margaret M Shead's interment is known only through family records and the location can be determined by other known interments of the family. In section B, rows 19 and 20 G and F that have no existing markers, there are approximately five unmarked plots.

Area cemeteries closest to Shead Ranch Cemetery

Mount Antioch, first recorded interment – 1860. Mount Antioch borders the central portion of the ranch, located halfway between the main portion and the two most northern sections, one reaching over into Hill County. Charles B Shead, his wife, and young child are interred here as well as members of the McKinney branch of the family. After Amanda died, William B Shead married widow M M J Elizabeth Wood. She is interred in Mount Antioch Cemetery beside two of her children. This small community centered around the Mount Antioch Baptist Church which still stands in its original location today. The cemetery and church property are bounded on the north by one of the ranch's northern sections.

SURVEY INFORMATION	
SURVEY NAME - MANSON SHIED	
GRANTEE NAME - Sheid, Manson	
ABSTRACT - 498	
ORIGINAL ACRES - 69	
PATENT INFORMATION: Archived Record	
PATENTEE NAME - Sheid, Manson (Heirs)	
DISTRICT - Robertson	
CLASSIFICATION - Robertson 1st	
FILE NUMBER - 001053	
PATENT DATE - 12 Sep 1862	
CERTIFICATE - 36/380	
PATENT NUMBER - 579	
PATENT VOLUME - 15	

Mount Calm Cemetery, about a half a mile northwest of Mount Antioch, is on land patented to Heirs of Manson Sheid and owned by William B Shead. Charles B Shead administered the property. The first interment recorded at this cemetery is in 1870. The town of Mount Calm originally bordered the cemetery. When railroad tracks were laid two miles north, the citizens began to relocate. The town now borders a large section of the original ranch land that stretched into Hill County.

Cassandra L Shead Coates (pictured right) and family are interred in this cemetery.

The land for Mount Calm Cemetery is recorded as donated to the town by J Kimmel, the father of the first child interred there. GLO records show it is on Limestone County Abstract 498, as part of the original Sheid holdings.

Prairie Hill Cemetery is located about a mile past the east end of the main portion of Shead Ranch. The first interment was in 1893. This cemetery was used by many people who lived and worked near the ranch. Several of the single family member interments in Shead Cemetery have more family members located here in later years. This cemetery borders a church and is in use to this day. The cemetery is well maintained.

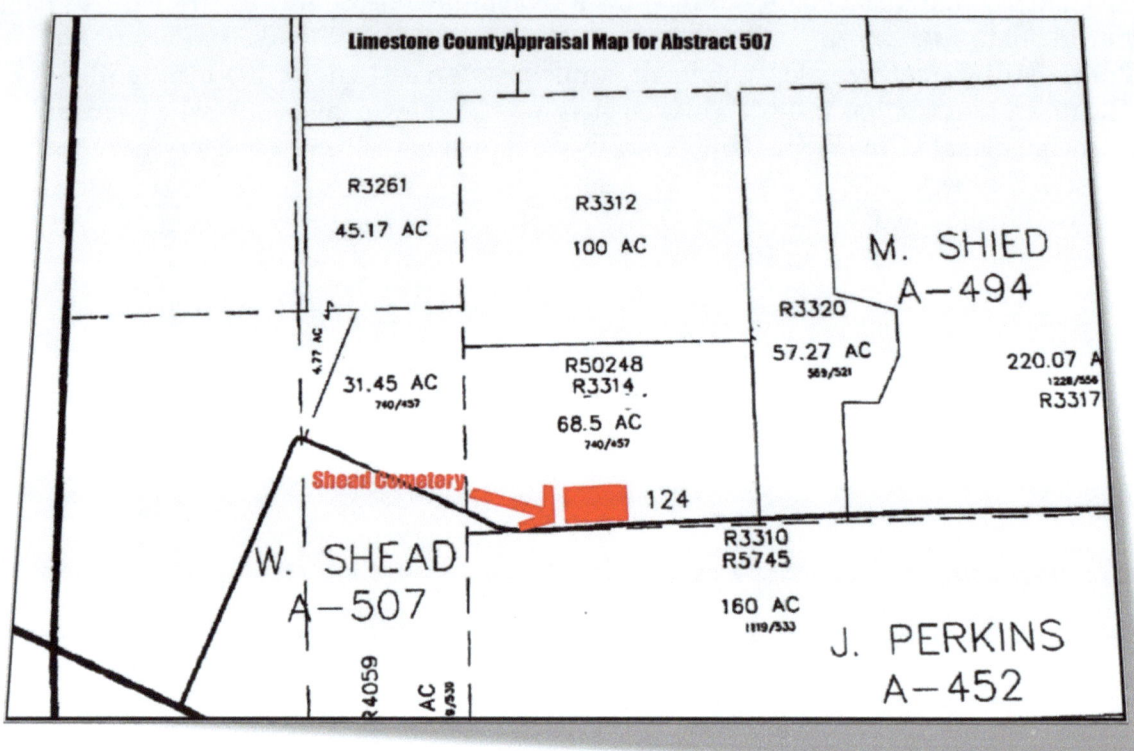

2014 GLO MAP

Division of the ranch depicting current day owner's boundaries along with original survey numbers for M. Shied (Manson Sheid) and W. Shead (William Robertson Shead).

Research and Preservation Notes

2013

Initial exploration September 2013 - Almost all headstones are overgrown. The view is daunting and still beautiful at sunrise. Three Shead family headstones are visible. Agnes and Manson H Shead, husband and wife, and Nancy Shead Sanderson. Agnes and Manson are pillar style monuments.

Located M. Brown monument inside an overgrown wrought iron fence. Counted markers inside maintained area of the Auberry Earls family section.

Gathered bits from shattered marble marker damaged by vehicle or mower by Auberry gate and grouped them at base, only legible word is "boy". Spotted some low concrete structure deep in brambles.

The amount of work needed to clear away brambles to document and photograph headstones is immeasurable today.

October 10 - Plotted boundary. Measured location of prominent monuments of Agnes and Manson H. Shead. Identified the concrete structures seen on my first visit as two crypts. Began graphing and photographing project. Documenting all bits of markers, lose stones etc. before anything is moved.

October 20 - Clearing and Survey: Cleared vines from monuments, cleared path past the pillars. Identified and graphed location of 36 monuments. Surprised to find a third crypt between the first two seen on a previous visit. Located second chain-link fenced area.

October 21, 2013 - Filed an application for historic designation for the cemetery with Texas State Historic Commission: Historic Cemeteries of Texas application. The commission is in downtown Austin, Texas, just a few blocks from the state capitol building, it is a historic structure surrounded by gardens of native plants. The application contains documents of both William's and Manson's activities during the Texas Revolution along with GLO certified documents for land grants denoting the boundaries of the cemetery. Pictures included in the application show the current condition of the cemetery, several markers, and list statistics concerning known interments.

October 21- Survey and Restoration: Located one buried marker (Alpha Donoho Smith). Marked it with reflective pole as it is in a current drive path toward the first chain-link gate. Graphed location of 6 markers. We located base for displaced monument and footstone of W. E. Buchanan. Returned them to their original location. Research results: "Boy" monument could be Luther Buchanan, Claudy E Cates, John T. Thompson, Hassie Earl Oliver or Charlie Thompson. Compiling earlier cemetery photographs for reference.

October 30 - Identified damaged "Boy" monument as Luther Buchanan from 1990 photo by MA Tarkington Johnson. Plotted location on map.

November 3 - Volunteer help today from Alex and Andy. By using a depth rod, Andy found buried markers of Austin Donoho and his grandchild, Hassie Earl Oliver. Alex cleaned and lowered surface soil around each.

The cemetery is on almost level ground, but the eastern portion has a mild slope and over the past hundred years has seen a shift. Most of the buried markers have been covered by soil that has drifted from the west. As these markers are on an incline, permanent restoration will require they be raised. These are home-made markers of concrete. Located and plotted markers of same family, William and Ida Buchanan. Marked location.

Unable to remove the tree that had collapsed on Buchanan family group monuments because our tools were stolen while we were away on an errand. Had an adventure looking for the thieves and talking to the Limestone sheriff's office. Photographed what was visible of the Buchanan monuments.

Located and graphed monument for M. E. Haden. Located base of monument believed to be Amanda Shead. The base has shifted and is tilted to the east.

November 13 - Neil Davis and friends locate and uncover the monument for John P Davis. They restore the monument's orientation and mark the area for future reference and restoration work. Neil provides the plot location for the cemetery map, a crucial step in preservation.

J P Davis Restoration Work & Photo by Neil Davis

November 20 - Located the monument for Amanda Shead and matched to broken base located immediately north of William R Shead. It is in four pieces. Cleaned, photographed and left in situ.

November 21 - Copied funeral records in Waco Genealogy library for two previously unknown burials in Shead Ranch Cemetery. Infants A. Janes and Lelia Mangrum.

December 2013 - Located burial record for Morris Sanderson, husband of Nancy Shead Sanderson and also Ludvick Beralek, Martin Beralek. Estimated Morris Sanderson is buried south of his wife. Headstones for Martin and Ludvick Beralek have not been noted on earlier surveys.

2014

February 2014 The cemetery is adopted as a community project by the Williams Creek Baptist Church Brotherhood. The church is located inside the south border of the main portion of the ranch. The Brotherhood's cleanup begins with removal of bramble bushes, uncovering several markers. They continue with the tremendous task of tree removal in March of the same year. The work conducted by Brotherhood members is performed with great care and respect. Each site is marked with a red flag or red pole and disturbance is kept to a minimum.

March 12 2014 Alex cleared trees around oldest of the three crypts, reassembled lid and positioned

fallen monument facing east. Filled in uneven ground between the three crypts. Cleaned and repositioned monument for the southern crypt. Located base of monument for Morris J Sanderson, husband of Nancy Shead Sanderson of Tennessee.

April 2014 Update from the Historic Commission, application is under review. Expectation was set that state budget cuts may delay the completion of the application for years.

April 2014 Completed older survey details, finalized plot locations. William's Creek Baptist Brotherhood continues their extraordinary labors.

April 2014 Davis family is working on plans for monument restoration. Discussed possible missing epitaph, estimated height of monument accounting for epitaph.

May 2014 William's Creek Baptist Brotherhood continues tree removal.

May 2014 Spring visit, photographed work in progress.

On the first visit in September 2013 the task of restoration was incalculable. The three markers visible in the above photograph are the one with the sleeping lamb atop it, and the matching markers of Mattie and Katheryn Shead, installed in 1950. The same monuments are in the foreground of the image below.

Preservation of the ranch cemetery will be an ongoing project. The key element accomplished by May 2014 was locating and plotting known interments. Family histories, funeral listings and death certificates were invaluable in compiling this information. I am hopeful that more facts, names and dates will be discovered in the years to come.

The preservation and documentation work continues.

Cemetery contact: SheadRanch@gmail.com

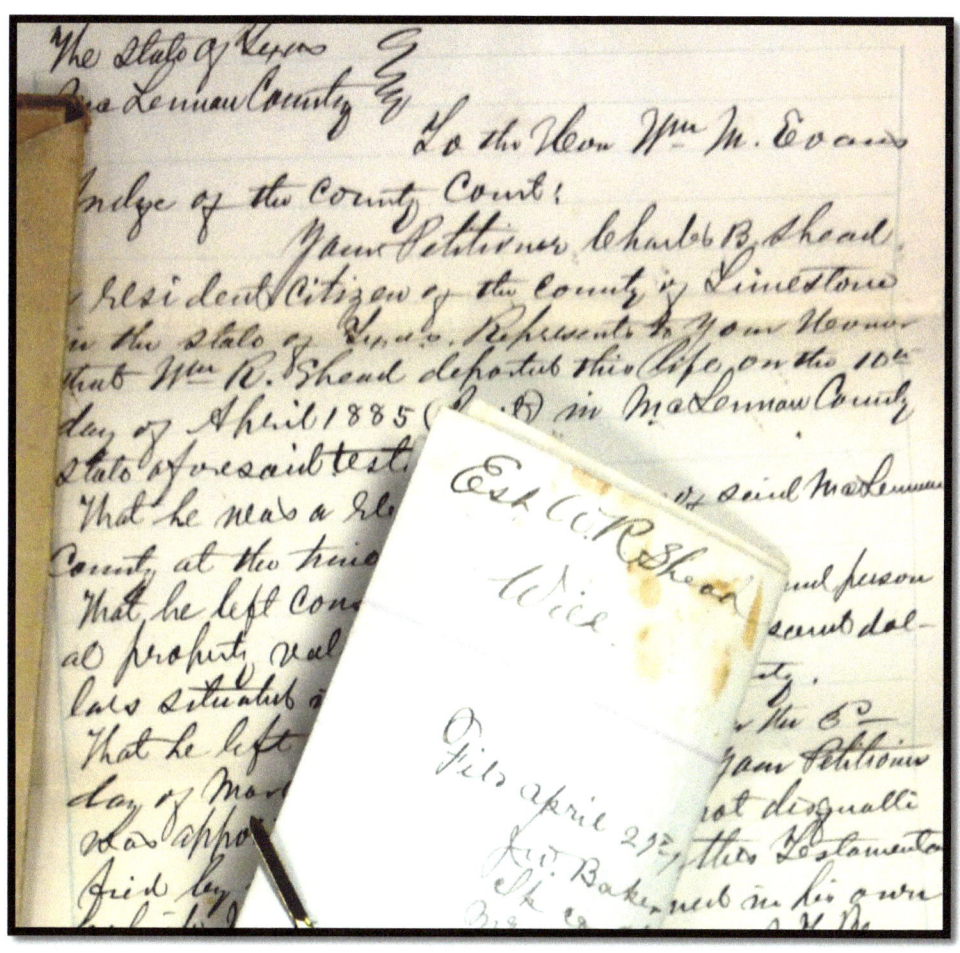

Marker Photographs

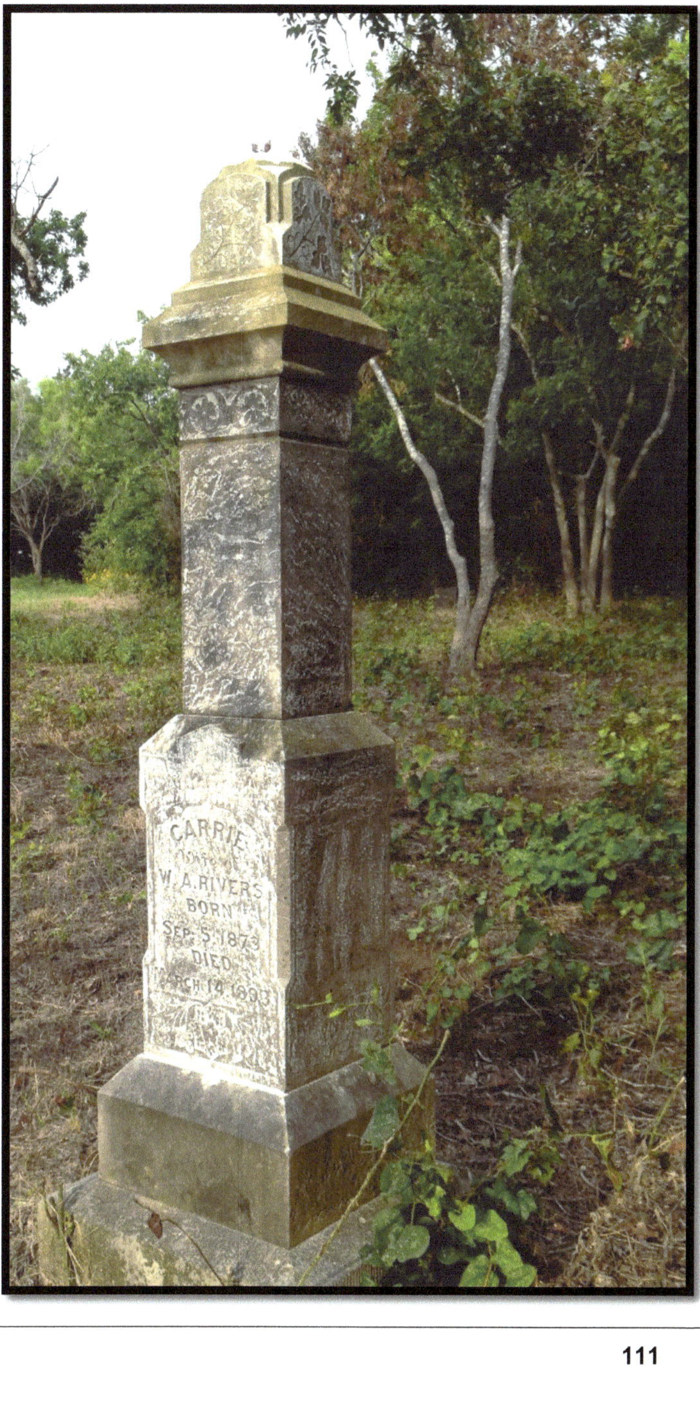
CARRIE
W. A. RIVERS
BORN
SEP. 5. 1873
DIED

H. C.
WIFE OF
CALVERY
BORN
DIED

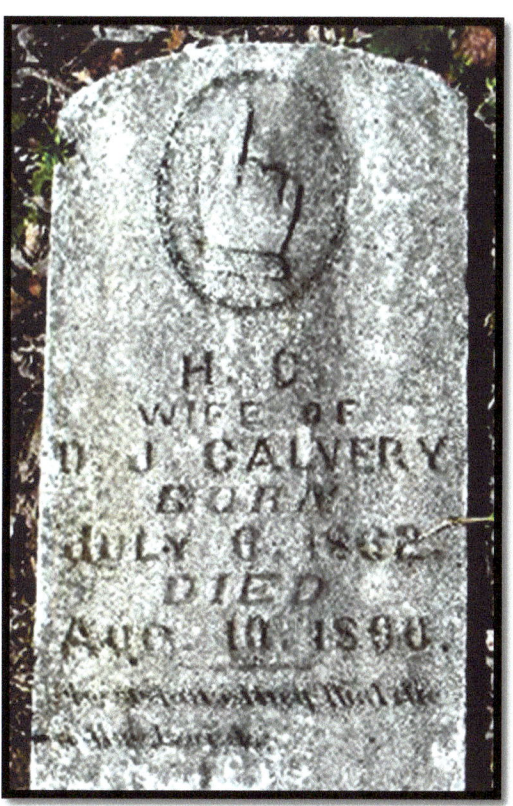

1990 Photo by
M A Tarkington Johnson

LELIA M. E.
DAU. OF
O. & S. A.
WATSON.
BORN
SEPT. 29, 1889
DIED
Nov. 23, 1890

Beautiful, lovely, she was given,
A fair bud to earth to
blossom in Heaven.

ETHEL P.
POLSON
Oct. 7, 1882
Nov. 14, 1925
AND INFANT

Bibliography:

Coldham, P. W. (1983). *Bonded passengers to America: Vol. 1*. Baltimore: Genealogical Publ. Co.

Jordan, Bruce, Jordan, Linda. "Shead Ranch Cemetery Limestone County, Texas" Interments. (Aug 10, 2003) Web. Dec 2013. http://www.interment.net/data/us/tx/limestone/shead/index.htm)

Loudoun County Deed Books, 1757-1785. Loudoun County Reels 1-6, Local Government Records Collection, The Library of Virginia, Richmond, Virginia.

Republic of Texas Claims, #196 Microfilm reel 95, Frames 98-100, Sheid, Manson enlistment. Texas State Library and Archives, Austin Texas.

Shedd, J. P. (1981). *The Shedd family of the southern states descended from James Shed of Loudoun County, Virginia*. Arlington, Va. (3705 North Woodstock St., Arlington 22207: J.P. Shedd.

Steele, H. (1925). A history of Limestone County, Texas, 1833-1860. Mexia, Tex: News Pub. Co.

Texas. (1888). *Limestone County, state of Texas*. Austin, Tex: General Land Office.

University of North Texas Libraries, The Portal to Texas History, http://texashistory.unt.edu; crediting UNT Libraries Government Documents Department, Denton, Texas.

United States. Soil Conservation Service and Texas Agricultural Experiment Station General Soil Map, Limestone County, Texas, Map, 1997; digital image, (http://texashistory.unt.edu/ark:/67531/metapth130304/ : accessed December 1, 2013).

Usry, J. M., & Central Texas Genealogical Society. (1974). *Fall and Puckett funeral records: Arranged alphabetically by names*. S.l.: Central Texas Genealogical Society.

Index

Alexander, Ida Cornelia
   Buchanan, Ida 61
Arnold, Willie C 61
Auberry, George Allen 63
Beacon, Maria Nancy 64
Bennett, Vernie S 23
Beralek, Jan 64, 65, 77
Beralek, Ludvick 65
Beralek, Marie 64
Beralek, Martin 65
Boykin, James Richard 65
Boykin, Jessie Lee 65, 66
Bradbury, Mattie Lee 63
Brown, J M 37
Brown, John Michael 66
Buchanan, W. E. 61
Buchanan, William M 61
Calvery, Doc J 67
Carey, Captain William 6
Carl, Thomas Robert 15
Cates, Claudy E 63
Chandler, Macon Frances
   Davis, Macon F C 70
Christian, Sophronia Swofford 67

Davis, John Phineas 67, 68
Donoho, Austin 58
Donoho, Mortimer 57, 58
Graham, Amanda
   Shead, A Graham 14, 15, 18, 37
Haden, Mary Elizabeth 33, 69
Hamlet, Cynthia 14
Henderson, Harriet Callie
   Calvery, Harriet 64
Henry, Joel G 47
Janes, A 69
Johnson, Garland 41
Jordan, Bruce 22
Jordan, Linda 22
Lasswell, Agnes A
   Shead, Agnes A Lasswell 16
Malone, Alpha 58, 59, 91
Mangrum, Lelia 69
McKinney, James Robert 42, 51
McKinney, John W 42
Morgan, Claudia V
   Thompson, Claudia Morgan 49
Mount Antioch 9
Mount Calm 9

Oliver, Hassie Earl 59
Patton, Mary E
    Sheid, Mary E Patton 14
Perez, Manual 69
Pitts, Ben 47
Polson, Bert Taylor 69
Polson, Ethel Pearl 69
Rivers, Carrie 70
Rivers, William Alfred 70
Robison, Anna L 53
Robison, Blanche Locke 53
Robison, Caroll B 53
Robison, Louis B 53
Robison, Pinkney Thomas 53
Sanderson, Morris J 45
Sanderson, William R 46
Shead, Agnes Lasswell 40
Shead, Amanda M
    Coates, Amanda M Shead 15
Shead, Cassandra L
    Coates, Cassandra Shead 15
Shead, Charles Baldwin 15, 19
Shead, James B 15, 19, 39
Shead, Katheryn McCall
    Johnson Katie M Shead 40, 41
Shead, Laura Jane
    Sanderson, Laura J Shead 15

Shead, Manson H 15, 19, 46
Shead, Margaret M 15, 38
Shead, Mary Ann
    Henry, Mary Ann Shead 15, 40
Shead, Mattie Amanda 27, 40
Shead, Nancy Matilda
    Nancy M Shead Sanderson 15, 45
Shead, William Robertson 5, 11, 14, 18, 37
Shed, James Austin 6, 11, 18
Sheid, Henry S 14
Sheid, James Manson 5, 14, 42
Sheid, Jane J
    McKinney, Jane J Sheid 14, 42, 59
Sheid, Jesse J 14
Sheid, Jesse L
    Renick, Jesse L Sheid 14
Sheid, Julius C 14, 43
Sheid, Manson 5, 14, 34
Sheid, Mary Clementine
    Gunn, Mary C Sheid 14
Sheid, Nancy
    Clark, Nancy Sheid 14
Sheid, Nancy Cora
    Willis, Nancy C Sheid 14
Sheid, Nancy M
    Carl, Nancy Sheid 14

Sheid, Sarah Coziah
    Camp, Sarah Coziah Sheid 14
Sheid, Selina
    Taylor, Selina Sheid 14
Sheid, Sibbel Robertson
    Robertson, Sibbel................................ 5
Sheid, William Thomas........................ 14
Sims, Margaret B.................................... 14
Stephenson , Matilda L
    Davis, Matilda L S............................ 67
Thompson, Charlie................................ 49
Thompson, Eugene A............................ 49
Thompson, John..................................... 49

Tillman, J C 70
Walker, Elihu B 51
Walker, Samuel H.................................. 51
Watson, Ada Pearl................................. 70
Watson, Lelia M E.................................. 70
Watson, Oliver 70
Watson, Samantha A............................. 70
Williams, William L............................... 71
Wood, Alice Letha 51
Wood, Martha 51
Wood, Thomas 51

www.ingramcontent.com/pod-product-compliance
Lightning Source LLC
Chambersburg PA
CBHW042020150426
43197CB00003B/87